Gems from the Jewelry Box

Gems from the Jewelry Box

God Loves You Most!

JEWELS PETRIE

Library of Congress Control Number:		2009900648
ISBN:	Hardcover	978-1-4415-0514-9
	Softcover	978-1-4415-0513-2

This book was printed in the United States of America.

To order additional copies of this book, contact:
Xlibris Corporation
1-888-795-4274
www.Xlibris.com
Orders@Xlibris.com
58034

CONTENTS

Shine: Let Your Living Water Flow

It Is You, Lord: You Are All I Need

The Rock: He Called to Me

I Look Up: Keep My Eyes on You

I Stand in Awe: How Can They Not Believe

To all people, saved or unsaved, in all nations. The ground at the foot of the cross is level. No matter who you are or what you have done, God loves you.

To my past and present mentors and those who believed in me before I ever believed in myself—my spiritual and earthly parents, my friends, and the old saints who poured into my life the Living Word.

For Christ's renown . . .

PREFACE

I am known to my friends as Jewels, but more important than who I am is who I believe in. I was inspired to begin writing these devotionals because of the great and mighty things God has done and what He has brought me through. It is my desire to share with the world the message of God's restoration and salvation through writing and musical worship.

Each of these gems, little nuggets of God's truth, was inspired by God's Holy Word or, metaphorically, the Jewelry Box. It is my hope to share how God manifested Himself in my life and became real to me so that, in turn, He will become more real to all who would read these pages.

I feel compelled to share my testimony, to share what God has done in my life to bring Him glory and honor. It is my prayer that, through these devotionals, every person reading would know that God cares for them deeply, and what He has done for me, He will do for anyone else.

I was the child of a single mother in the '70s and was adopted at the age of thirteen. I acted out in almost every way imaginable including drinking, doing drugs, and having sex during my preteen years prior to my adoption. My first suicide attempt was at about age twelve. I was trying desperately to numb the pain of my early childhood.

I carried all of my dysfunctional behavior and pain from my youth well into my adulthood years and into my adult relationships. I have overcome many trials and tribulations, including the infidelity and abandonment by my ex-husband and the death of my best friend, only with God's strength and by His grace.

It is my prayer that this collection of devotionals will inspire and challenge other believers to strengthen and deepen their relationship with God. It is also my prayer that any unsaved readers would turn to the Rock in their time of need and call upon the name of the Lord to be saved. Remember, He loves you most!

ACKNOWLEDGMENTS

Cordie, my spiritual mother, you started off being my friend at a time in my life when I was completely broken and very much at the end of myself. You planted the seeds, and God took care of the rest. I thank you for your love, the love only a mother can give. God will bless you beyond measure for the blessing you have been to me. Thanks for all the continued support and encouragement along with the editing and fabulous photography for this project. Wonderful pictures, Mother! You have spurred me along countless times since our meeting and have pulled me up the hill even when I wanted to stay right where I was. I love you, Mother!

Darlene, thanks for always supporting me during my darkest hours and my highest mountaintops. You have been a true friend every step of the way, as you have been there for me through all the tears, laughter, singing, ministering, praying, heartbreaking pain, joy, and healing. You continue to watch me grow, sprout wings, fall, and sometimes even manage to fly, encouraging me at all points in between and along the way. Oh, Wise One, you help me blossom more and more.

Kerry and Mariely, thank you both for all the support and time that you guys invest in me—musically, spiritually, and personally. Both of your ministries changed and continue to change my life and deepen my walk. I appreciate all the kindness and love of Christ that you both have shown me.

Special thanks to you, Kerry, for all your help in bringing God's music to life and for all your numerous contributions on the CD project, *Gems from the Jewelry Box: The Reason.* Thank you for being cowriter on "Save Me" (take me to the bridge, Crespo), being producer and arranger, for playing all the instruments (especially those horn and upright bass lines I love), for singing some of my background vocals, and for all the work you have done throughout the very time-consuming process of recording, mixing, etc. It's time, brother! I appreciate the opportunities that you have given me. They mean more to me than you will ever know, and I am so grateful to God and to you.

Special thanks to you, Mariely, for your support and sacrifice as well. Never underestimate who you are and what you do. You are vital to God's plan, Sister!

We still have some planting to do y'all! I know the Casa kids have not forgotten our theme song.

Who all of you are has an immeasurable impact on who I am becoming!

INTRODUCTION

Shortly before God began nudging me to write and e-mail the following devotionals, He began blessing me with melodies and lyrics. The soon-to-be-released CD, *Gems from the Jewelry Box: The Reason* (cowritten, produced, arranged, and recorded by Kerry Crespo), is a compilation of original songs that is the counterpart of these devotionals. Thus, I have divided this book into sections and listed the devotionals under the song titles that apply. My contact information and information regarding the CD is available at www.myspace.com/gemsfromthejewelrybox.

The Reason

You Are the Answer

My Earliest Memory

It happened when I was two and a half years old. I watched from the steps as an argument erupted between my mother and her boyfriend. I can still hear the screaming followed by the violence. I vividly remember running up the steps into a bedroom with yellow curtains and a white comforter on the bed, crying and terrified. Sadly, I can remember the violent beating that I endured after he finished with my mother.

She would confirm my earliest memory many years later. A couple of years ago, my aunt also confirmed that she took us in for a time because she found marks on me, at some point, during my mother's relationship with this man whose name I will never forget.

This experience has been with me forever. It's not like it suddenly came rushing back when I became an adult. This memory used to replay in my mind like a video, over and over again, constantly reinforcing that I was a victim—powerless, mistreated, unloved, and helpless.

I used to think that, if only I could get over it—*it* being all the things that happened to me as a child—then I would be okay. I used to think that, if somehow I could make sense of the events of my youth and understand them, then somehow this understanding would change things. I believed it would change me—who I was and how I viewed myself.

I used to play the "If Only" game. It goes something like this: if only my earliest memory was something happy, if only my biological father did not leave when I was so young, if only she protected me from that man and the others, if only she did not leave me alone behind closed doors to suffer more abuse, if only we stayed in the church, if only she did not get married, if only she didn't give me up for adoption, if she only loved me, if only he could have loved me unconditionally, if only . . .

Then, Satan's mind game was interrupted. I found God, one January day, in 2005. He had been waiting patiently, keeping His hand upon my life and watching me flounder and fall on my face repeatedly until I was ready to give in to Him. He was waiting for me to give up on trying to make sense of my senseless past, find love from people who were not capable of giving it, and cover up the pain with food, drugs, alcohol, and men.

Only God has been able to reveal that I am more than the circumstances of my victimized youth and adulthood, and that I am more than anything that has ever happened in my past or will happen to me in the future. He has shown me that I am no longer abused, unprotected, and unloved.

The funny thing is that He has begun to answer the if onlys. Had I not gone through everything and had the pain of the first thirty-three to thirty-four years of my life not been so tragically intense, I would not be a testimony to God's goodness, grace, love, mercy, compassion, and life-changing power. I would not be sitting here at 4:15 AM on a Saturday morning, writing this to encourage you that God is able to move you beyond anything in your life that you think you need to get over.

God is able to heal you, and He loves you more than you could ever imagine. No matter what you are going through and no matter what you've gone through, let Him speak to your heart. Let Him elevate you above all your circumstances—past, present, and future. No matter what you've done in your past to cover up your pain, He can and will forgive you whether you were the abuser or the abused, the victim or one who victimized. He can change your life—all of it—your thinking, your heart, your mind, your feelings, and your circumstance. He can erase your sins and renew you.

There is a scripture that changed my life forever. I pray that you let this passage speak *life* into you, and that you hear the whisper of God's still-small voice.

> The Spirit of the Sovereign LORD is on me, because the LORD has anointed me to preach good news to the poor. He has sent me to bind up the brokenhearted, to proclaim freedom for the captives and release from darkness for the prisoners, to proclaim the year of the LORD's favor and the day of vengeance of our God, to comfort all who mourn, and provide for those who grieve in Zion—
> to bestow on them a crown of beauty
> instead of ashes,
> the oil of gladness
> instead of mourning,
> and a garment of praise
> instead of a spirit of despair.
> They will be called oaks of righteousness,
> a planting of the LORD
> for the display of His splendor (Isaiah 61:1-3, NIV)

God blessed me with a song called "The Reason" based upon this very scripture. It was one of those songs that just came out of nowhere. First, it was the words that just came pouring out of me. Then a melody came. This song really was part of the healing process. They all seem to be.

Jesus came to bind up your broken heart and to set you free. You no longer have to be a prisoner to your past, present, or future, to your circumstance, or to your pain. You are favored, and God will comfort you. He wants to make you an oak of righteousness and fill your life with beauty and happiness.

> No, in all these things we are more than conquerors through Him who loved us. For I am convinced that neither death nor life, neither angels nor demons, neither the present nor the future, nor any powers, neither height nor depth, nor anything else in all creation, will be able to separate us from the love of God that is in Christ Jesus our Lord. (Romans 8:37-39, NIV)

But God, What About Me?

What is that scripture where Paul talks about "doing that which I do not want to do"? It's in Romans.

Sometimes it is so hard to say no to the things that God does not want us to do or things He wants us to give up or, likewise, do the things we should. You know what I mean? We all have our own "things."

Hosea 6:7 reads, "Like Adam, they have broken the covenant—they were unfaithful to me there."

The *they*, in this scripture, is referring to the people of Israel and their disobedience. They had their thing, and it was idol worship. These were God's chosen people who had witnessed His goodness, His provision, and His deliverance. Yet still, they broke their covenant and chose to bow down to some thing rather than submitting to the only One worthy. They were no different from Adam.

Adam teaches us that even someone so close to God, who was given everything, can be consumed with temptation to the point where he would choose to give in to his flesh, his wants, and his desires and lose all that God had for him. Can you imagine having that perfect communion with God and then losing it?

Look at David's apple. Her name was Bathsheba. Even David was overcome by his flesh and fell, and he was a man after God's own heart.

Time and time again, you see it throughout the lives of God's people. God's chosen and anointed ones all had their things. So do I.

Recently, I found myself reverting back to some pre-embryonic, less-than-baby Christian state. I asked God as I was wrestling with Him about my thing—"But what about me? What about what I want?"—in a moment of frustration, tiredness, and weakness in my own recent personal battle.

Sure enough, Mark 8:34 was right there, popping off the page to answer my whining plea. "Then He called the crowd to Him along with His disciples and said: 'If anyone would come after me, he must deny himself [his thing, his wants, his desires] and take up his cross [submission to God's will] and follow me.'" Ouch! "For whoever wants to save his life will lose it, but whoever loses his life for me and for the Gospel will save it." Double ouch!

But God . . . God always makes a way for repentance, for atonement, for forgiveness, and for restoration. We are all human and live within these earthly, flesh-ridden tents provided to house the Spirit, which really is our only source of power to overcome and control it.

Even when dying to "it" seems almost an impossible task, God gives us the promise of self-control, and it is one of the fruits of the Spirit (see Galatians 5). It is time to exercise some spiritual self-control and lay "it" down at the foot of the cross. At the same time, I need to take up my own and submit once again to the Father who knows best and loves me most.

So for anyone else out there, who may be battling with your "thing" or your "it," I would encourage you to focus on Him, focus on His grace, His mercy, His compassion, His faithfulness, and His Power. Remember, through every season and every struggle, He is the reason!

Pain Because Your Time Has Come!

Check out this scripture in John.

> I tell you the truth, you will weep and mourn while the world rejoices. You will grieve, but your grief will turn to joy. A woman giving birth to a child *has pain because her time has come*; but when her baby is born she forgets the anguish because of her joy that a child is born into the world. So with you: Now is your time of grief, but I will see you again and you will rejoice, and no one will take away your joy. (John 16:20-22, NIV; emphasis added)

The context of this passage is right after Jesus promises the Comforter, the Counselor (verses 5-16). He tells the disciples that He is leaving them and going to the Father. Jesus tells them, in verse 12, "I have more to say to you, more than you can now bear."

Keep in mind that this is only hours away from His death and yet, at the same time, three days from His resurrection. His disciples asked each other, "What does He mean 'you will see me no more'?"

So Jesus sees that they are asking one another and jumps in to tell them the above passage and then proceeds to tell them (in verse 23), "In that day, you will no longer ask me anything. I tell you the truth that my Father will do whatever you ask in my name."

So many things strike me in that passage. Specifically, I want to focus on *has pain because her time has come!*

Jesus knew the pain He was about to endure and the physical, emotional, and spiritual agony of taking on the sins of the world. The time had come for Him to fulfill His destiny and His purpose.

Our destiny, whatever it is that God has burned in us to do for Him, will come with some pain and at a cost. Just like in Matthew 8:18-22, Jesus tells a teacher of the law that He has no place even to lay His head. Jesus did not offer security in earthly material things. When another disciple told Jesus that he had to go bury his father first, Jesus did not accept his excuse. (There are several possible meanings of the last part of the scripture, and we will save that debate for some other day.) The point is that you cannot really say you want to follow Christ if you are concerned with your comfort, your convenience, your agenda, and you are interested in making excuses. Sometimes doing the thing you are called to do may not fit into your schedule, your timeline, or your expectations.

I have to honestly tell you that the songs God blesses me with come only after or in the midst of great pain and suffering. It is the stuff no one else sees but God and me. He collects all of my many tears, and to steal a popular catchphrase, there is a lot of time spent going through it to get to it. However, at the end of it is the birth of something wonderful. There is the infilling in the deepest part of me with His joy that no one can take away! Are you willing to take the time to go through the pain to get to the joy, which cannot be taken away?

Comfort and Freedom

Her name was Baby E. She was born somewhere around the twenty-fourth week of her mother's pregnancy, which made her a micropreemie. Micro is exactly what she was.

Her head was the size of a baseball with hands so small and delicate—about the size of the tip of my thumb. Her skin was mocha-caramel with some crème on top and very fragile.

She was beautiful with her little bit of black hair and her cute little toes and nose in spite of all the equipment that we had attached to her precious little face to keep her alive. She was born with her eyes still fused shut, but when they finally opened, she had the most amazing little black marbles that looked up at me. I know she saw me although I'm sure I was blurry.

She saw me everyday, except for my days off from being a NICU (Neonatal Intensive Care Unit) nurse, for about the first four to five months of her little life. I loved her.

When she was finally old enough to be held, I would sing to her and rock her for hours. Her setbacks were painful, but her victories were glorious. She was a miracle.

She should have died many different times from the many different issues that micros face, but not her. She was a fighter and all full of spunk. She went home with her parents after a long hospital stay against all odds. She was the first of many micros that I would care for during my NICU tour of duty, and she was unforgettable for so many reasons.

She should not have been able to see from the infection that basically ate away most of her occipital (sight control center) lobe in her brain, but I will never forget the day when her parents brought her back to visit me a couple of years later. She was wearing her little glasses and very much able to see. She should not have been able to walk or talk either, but she did all those things and more.

—

Her mother and I caught up about a year ago on the phone, and I heard all the good reports of how school-aged E had continual improvements in her development. We were never able to arrange our schedules so I could actually see E, but I was satisfied to know that she had made it and was growing up like every other special-needs kid in America. I then lost track of her mother's number.

When I was at work the other day, an old friend who actually is biologically a distant cousin of mine from the NICU called. She was telling me all about how E's mother had another baby a couple months ago. This nurse had ended up taking care of their second-born daughter in the NICU, born only a few weeks early, and updating me on their lives. She updated me on E and how pretty she was with her long black curly hair and how she was a happy girl—laughing and smiling.

When she said that E had died, it felt like the world stopped for a minute. It was like casual conversation that just slammed into a brick wall. She just said it so plainly. "E died. She's dead."

Nothing can express the flood of emotions that overtook my heart when she uttered those few words. The tears and disbelief came. My friend tried to comfort me.

She gave me the phone number of E's mother who was trying to track me down. Before I called her, I was so concerned about what comforting words I could possibly speak at such a time. Little did I know that God's glory would shine in such a moment as this.

I called. I told her I was so sorry for her loss. I then told her how much I had loved her daughter too, and she said she knew this.

Then God . . . She started expressing her gratitude over the time that she had with E. She said she was so glad to have the ten years with E that she did. I was so struck by her gratefulness. Her thanksgiving had comforted me instead of the other way around.

I am drawn back to Isaiah 61:1-3 (NIV) repeatedly: "To comfort all who mourn and provide for those who grieve." Jesus quoted these very words in Luke 4, proclaiming that he was the fulfillment of that scripture in Isaiah. *He* is the only one who can truly bind up our broken hearts no matter what they are broken from—whether it is from death, broken relationships, or loss. *He* is the only freedom from captivity, whatever may be holding us captive, whether it is related to our emotions, finances, circumstances, past, present, or future.

Jesus also said, in John 14:18 (KJV), "I will not leave you comfortless: I will come to you." He promises that He won't leave us comfortless.

Jesus was speaking about how the Comforter would come to his apostles, and that He would abide with us forever. He is always with us; we just have to recognize Him and His power.

—

As I prepare myself spiritually to attend E's viewing and funeral, I am reminded that we are not promised tomorrow or even the next breath . . . But we are promised comfort through the Holy Spirit and freedom through Jesus Christ.

Amen!

RAINBOWS AND GOD'S COVENANT

Rainbows . . . What are they really made of, why do we see them, and where is the end of one? The internet has an overwhelming amount of endless information on rainbows. Do a quick search, and you will find links to additional information on related topics like sundogs, moonbows, halos, and circumhorizontal arcs. Just one click can provide hours of light-reading fun.

I can tell you that science will explain God's glorious physical manifestation of His covenant in terms of refraction, cirrus clouds, latitude and the sun's position, and it being behind you or certain amounts of degrees high in the sky or low to the horizon blah blah blah—science. My nursing mind loves science, so don't misunderstand.

However, what happens when science cannot explain the miraculous? What if you see a rainbow, but the research says that it is scientifically impossible? What if you saw a rainbow in the clouds, and there was no rain? Would you call it a miracle?

The nurse in me could spend hours researching the ROYGBIV phenomena, and truth be told, I did. However, most things of God and His beauty just cannot be explained at all.

MEPHIBOSHETH

In talking to a friend recently, something was mentioned about a relative of Saul who was brought to the palace. I did not know this Old Testament story he was referring to. Then, a few days later I was reading a book and there was this story again about a son of Jonathan, son of Saul. It seemed that God was trying to get my attention.

Everyday there are new treasures to be found in the Jewelry Box. Mephibosheth and his story is one of them. His story is found in 2 Samuel, chapter 9 (NIV):

> David asked, "Is there anyone still left of the house of Saul to whom I can show kindness for Jonathan's sake?" Now there was a servant of Saul's household named Ziba. They called him to appear before David, and the king said to him, "Are you Ziba?" "Your servant," he replied. The king asked, "Is there no one still left of the house of Saul to whom I can show God's kindness?" Ziba answered the king, "There is still a son of Jonathan; he is crippled in both feet." "Where is he?" the king asked. Ziba answered, "He is at the house of Makir son of Ammiel in Lo Debar."
>
> So King David had him brought from Lo Debar, from the house of Makir son of Ammiel. When Mephibosheth son of Jonathan, the son of Saul, came to David, he bowed down to pay him honor.
>
> David said, "Mephibosheth!" "Your servant," he replied. "Don't be afraid," David said to him, "for I will surely show you kindness for the sake of your father Jonathan. I will restore to you all the land that belonged to your grandfather Saul, and you will always eat at my table." Mephibosheth bowed down and said, "What is your servant, that you should notice a dead dog like me?"

—

Then the king summoned Ziba, Saul's servant, and said to him, "I have given your master's grandson everything that belonged to Saul and his family. You and your sons and your servants are to farm the land for him and bring in the crops, so that your master's grandson may be provided for. And Mephibosheth, grandson of your master, will always eat at my table."

(Now Ziba had fifteen sons and twenty servants.) Then Ziba said to the king, "Your servant will do whatever my lord the king commands his servant to do."

So Mephibosheth ate at David's table like one of the king's sons. Mephibosheth had a young son named Mica, and all the members of Ziba's household were servants of Mephibosheth. And Mephibosheth lived in Jerusalem, because he always ate at the king's table, and he was crippled in both feet.

If you turn back to 2 Samuel 4:4, it says that he was only five when he heard the news regarding the death of Jonathan, his father, and of Saul, his grandfather. His nurse had picked him up to flee, but there was some sort of a fall that occurred. When he fell, he became crippled in both legs. Mephibosheth was abandoned from a very early age and would have needed others to care for him.

I am guessing that Mephibosheth may have felt some serious anxiety over being summoned by the new king. I can only imagine the sheer terror when he arrived to meet with David. David, who I always imagine to be very discerning, quieted Mephibosheth's fear immediately. The first thing David said to him was "Do not fear."

David wanted to give him blessings, not do him harm. Mephibosheth had no basis for his fear despite his preconceived notions. I can picture it in my head, the shock of Mephibosheth, when he finds out David's true intentions—to bless him and provide restoration. David's compassion and loyalty to God's anointed also shines through and shows the integrity that a true leader must display.

Mephibosheth responds with a why me. He even goes so far as to call himself a dead dog. He must have felt so unworthy or he never would have referred to himself in this way. He was crippled and not able to be productive or self-sufficient, but God would provide the way.

Has there ever been a time when you felt unworthy like Mephibosheth? Ever feel afraid of a situation because you felt inadequate? Is your self-perception keeping you crippled when God is trying to provide you with everything you need?

I am here to tell you that, through Jesus Christ, if you are a believer, you are made worthy by His blood! So receive that gift. It is not earned!

No physical imperfection and no self-imposed inadequacy can hinder the hand of the Lord from blessing you or moving in your life if you let Him. You may look in the mirror and think, *I'm too fat, I'm too skinny,* or *I'm not good enough.* The "I'm This" or "I'm That" game, fill in your own blank, is a lie from the pit of hell. Let Him define you, work through you, and change you. What does He tell you? Who does He say you are?

There is nothing that you can do to make God love you more except give up and give in to Him! You can turn over your insecurities to Him and let Him do the work in your life and to make the way for the blessing, but you must surrender to Him.

You are not a dead dog! You are a highly favored child of the Almighty!

RELIGION OR RELATIONSHIP

As for you, son of man, your countrymen are talking together about you by the walls and at the doors of the houses, saying to each other, "Come and hear the message that has come from the Lord." My people come to you, as they usually do, and sit before you to listen to your words, but they do not put them into practice. With their mouths they express devotion, but their hearts are greedy for unjust gain. Indeed, to them you are nothing more than one who sings love songs with a beautiful voice and plays an instrument well, for they hear your words but do not put them into practice.

—Ezekiel 33:30-32

This chapter actually starts Ezekiel's message of hope and restoration. This gem, in Ezekiel, really struck me particularly in verse 32—how they hear your words and do not put them into practice.

The people were hearing and not doing, not entering into relationship, just like today. People are no different, and people are tired of religion. I began to reflect upon why.

Just like in the days of Ezekiel, people don't want to hear you profess your devotion to God and then see you live some other way contrary to what you say. TV has spread the downfall of many a "religious" man whose greed has been displayed for all nations to see. It is easy to talk, but talk is cheap. Actions speak louder than words! *They scream!*

Where is your heart? What are your motives? Are you singing a beautiful love song or playing an instrument well, and yet your life and walk do not reflect Christ? Your life is a living testimony to your personal relationship with God. So how are you living it?

Save Me

Let This Flesh Be Dead

New Wineskin

It is no accident that some of the best times recently have been followed by the worst. This past week, only a couple of days after I saw a rainless rainbow, I was going through some things that really kind of scared me. This past week seemed to be a battle for my mind and for my very life. Call it an attack or spiritual warfare or call it being tried and tested. You can call it whatever you want. It was horrible and worse than any depression I have ever known—worse than the darkest times of my life to date—and there have been some pretty dark times.

I had written an e-mail intended for my closest friends that never got sent. In retrospect, I should have sent it, or talked to someone sooner, as I felt very isolated and alone in my battle. I knew there was something very wrong within me but was too scared to tell anyone.

I will share a little of what I was going through only to then share of God's faithfulness and how He really did bring me out.

Here is the e-mail:

> SOS—I'm having some issues over here at 609 . . .

> Right now, I am craving a cigarette, a drink . . . I will stop at that, and there really is no need for me to go into why because it is simply my lack of faith that has brought me to this horrible place tonight. I think I believe in the promises of the Almighty, but when the waves come, my actions say differently. I'm jumping out of the boat and sinking straight to the bottom.

> I mean, there have been times I have found myself smoking my pen in church or at work. Right now, this is different! This is not like my pen is in my mouth because of old habits.

Tonight, as I sit here fighting my way through this attack, I can honestly say my flesh wants to go buy a pack of my old cigs. I want to smoke them all with a great bottle of white wine or a nice bottle of expensive champagne, then take the black car out, and zip down the highway at 120 mph. I could take off for the shore, or some other distant destination, and disappear for a few days. None of you would know . . .

However, that is the deception of sin and self-destructive behaviors. It seems like it would be so easy to hide, but you can never hide from God because He always knows. He never slumbers, and He never sleeps. Even if I did take off, I would still be taking my mess with me. Even if I did have a drink or the whole bottle, eventually, I would wake up, and it would be even worse.

Sometimes those old habits and the way you were used to dealing with things in the world pop back up. It is no coincidence that God led me to Mark 2:22 (NIV), "And no one pours new wine into old wineskins. If he does, the wine will burst the skins, and both the wine and the wineskins will be ruined. No, he pours new wine into new wineskins."

Maybe God has allowed all of this to happen today to show me that I still have some things to work through or, rather, that He has some things to work out in me. I still have to find new ways to deal with life without all the self-destruction. Maybe it is to remind me that it is only by God's grace that I have been delivered, and that His faithfulness will see me through. So please pray for me as I pray for you, that I can surrender to the process and not surrender to the old wineskin way of doing things.

I thank God that He kept His hand upon me through this crisis, and I did not do anything stupid except that I did not ask for the help of my fellow saints sooner.

I was really ready to head over to the local psych ward and check-in for a few days because I felt like I was really losing my mind, but that would not have been the answer either.

There is something about crying out to God in those dark places where you are aching for the least little glimmer of light—when your pain is pouring forth from the very depths of your soul and you can't open your mouth to scream. He remains faithful, and even in our darkness, His consuming fire shines. Even in our pain, He is the Balm of Gilead.

See that you do not refuse Him who speaks. For if they did not escape who refused Him who spoke on earth, much more shall we not escape if we turn away from Him who speaks from heaven, whose voice then shook the earth; but now He has promised, saying, "Yet once more I shake not only the earth, but also heaven." Now this, "Yet once more," indicates the removal of those things that are being shaken, as of things that are made, that the things which cannot be shaken may remain. Therefore, since we are receiving a kingdom which cannot be shaken, let us have grace, by which we may serve God acceptably with reverence and godly fear. For our God is a consuming fire. (Hebrews 12:25-29, NKJV)

Because of the Lord's great love we are not consumed, for his compassions never fail. They are new every morning; great is your faithfulness. (Lamentations 3:22-23, NIV)

I cry out to God Most High, to God, who fulfills his purpose for me. He sends from heaven and saves me, rebuking those who hotly pursue me; Selah . . . God sends his love and his faithfulness. (Psalms 57:2-3, NIV)

It was an exhausting process, and the timing was not obvious to me until after it was all over. I was to minister in song "The Reason," a song that God had blessed me with about a year earlier that Sunday. "The Reason" means so much more now, more than ever before! My prayer, at the time, was that—as I ministered its message—I would actually be able to sing and not cry the entire way through it. I wanted everyone listening to know that there is restoration through Jesus, and that He wants to bind up every broken heart. I wanted everyone to see that He can change your life.

He really did bring me out and brought me through—to this other side. God blessed me with a new song called "Save Me" that was birthed out of this painful attack. The chorus very simply says, "Save me from myself." I think God let me get to the end of myself in yet another way through this experience. The only way to save ourselves is to acknowledge that we cannot, and that only Christ can really save us.

While I did not know what would await me here, on this new shore, I know that, somehow, the events of those days changed me forever. I can also attest that there have been other times, similar to this, when I have been made into a new wineskin again, changed for His purpose. Sometimes, I still struggle to rest in Him and His faithfulness!

No matter what you are going through, just know that He really is the reason, the answer, and our power through every season in life. No matter how bad it may seem at the time, He is our hope!

Let's Talk about Sex

Do I have your attention? Did that little chemical pop in your brain happen, instantly and involuntarily, just from reading those three little letters—s-e-x? The world is talking plenty about sex, and the media and marketing agencies know about that little chemical pop. And guess what? They feed it.

They know that, once that pop happens, they have your attention, and very consciously, you are in tune to it. It may be an overt advertisement with scantily clad men or women or a song with lyrics that are way too suggestive. They may use a more subtle tactic like sexual innuendo in conversations on both the big and little screens. Sex is everywhere unless you closely guard what you allow into your mind through your five senses.

Don't worry though! There is no need for pearls to clutch because I really do not want to talk about sex. I just wanted to prove my point and get your attention.

I actually want to talk about purity. No one else seems to be.

I've never gotten a devotional on it, I've never heard a sermon or Bible study on it, and even the local Christian bookstore has little reading to offer on it, and that may be because very few authors are writing about it. There are books available that say don't have sex, which are mostly aimed at teens, and offer very little guidance on how to fight a very real battle to remain pure—a concept that extends way beyond any physical or mental sexual act.

Whether you are single, married, or anywhere in between, God calls us to purity of thought and deed for both inner and outer purity. If our lives are to be living sacrifices, that means God wants all of us, not just some parts of us. He wants all of us, even those hidden parts that we think no one else knows about.

People in marital relationships, you still have eyes and, most importantly, a holy covenant before God, committing to your spouse. Your call to purity is important and vital because it affects you, your spouse, your kids, and most importantly, your relationship with the Almighty. Be aware and on guard at all times!

To those who are single, we have a tendency to think that looking won't hurt. However, what does God say about looking at a person lustfully? We think that somehow, because there is no ring on our finger, we have freedom that our married friends don't have. However, it's not okay to break your neck, looking at the hottie (whatever that is for you) that just passed by. I would challenge you that God has that finger wrapped with His love, and His covenant to you, with you. He is our first husband (see Isaiah 54). Please don't fall into the trap, thinking that what you do when you are single will not carry over into a marriage union. It will!

This is why we must protect our eyes, ears, hearts, bodies, and ultimately, our very souls because that is what hangs in the balance. That scripture about God giving people over to the lustful desires of their hearts should stop us dead in our tracks and make us all pause. Our glorious Maker gave us free will, and He will let us choose sin. Infidelity and sexual addiction are very real problems infecting the very core of our society. The enemy is busy!

Purity is not everywhere and really not anywhere at all. You must seek it out should you choose to honor God with your mind, body, spirit, and soul!

Does God's command for purity match your level of obedience to that command?

> Do not rebuke an older man harshly, but exhort Him as if he were your father. Treat younger men as brothers, older women as mothers, and younger women as sisters, with absolute purity. (1 Timothy 5:1-2)

> Do not be hasty in the laying on of hands, and do not share in the sins of others. Keep yourself pure. (1 Timothy 5:22)

Matthew 5:8 says, "Blessed are the pure in heart . . ." How pure is yours? There are Seven Woes found in Matthew 23. Jesus was concerned about purity not in terms of sexuality, if you look at the scripture literally, but one could apply it to this very topic as well. In verse 24, we see that the Pharisees were so concerned of their outer purity but had lost their inner purity. They were concerned with spiritual appearances.

It matters what choices you make! Jesus cares if you choose to break your neck, if you show too many teeth, if your eyes linger too long in a place they don't belong, or if you indulge in self-gratification. (Okay, pearl clutch, but it needed to be said.) It doesn't matter what you portray to others if the condition of your heart is filled with sin and lust.

God cares about what you do, what you watch, and what you listen to, not just what you say! So the question becomes how. Psalm 119:9 asks and answers this very question: "How can a young man keep his way pure? By living according to your Word!"

God wants our minds to be renewed, and His Word is part of that renewal process. Hide His Word so deeply within your heart, so that you may not sin, so that your eyes don't lead you where you don't want to go—into the valley of sinful separation.

God wants us to be pure. Have you really sought out what that means for you? Purity is a choice that is made moment to moment, second to second! His Word is a mighty weapon in the fight for purity, and I pray you all ingest it today. Remember, He is coming back for a church that is spotless and blameless, and we make up that church.

CODEPENDENCY

So they went to the king and spoke to him about his royal decree: "Did you not publish a decree that during the next thirty days anyone who prays to any god or man except to you, O king, would be thrown into the lions' den?" The king answered, "The decree stands—in accordance with the laws of the Medes and Persians, which cannot be repealed." Then they said to the king, "Daniel, who is one of the exiles from Judah, pays no attention to you, O king, or to the decree you put in writing. He still prays three times a day." When the king heard this, he was greatly distressed; he was determined to rescue Daniel and made every effort until sundown to save him.
—Daniel 6:12-14, NIV

How many times do we have people in our lives that we care about whom we are determined to rescue, and we become just like the king, so greatly distressed? We want to rescue them from their choices, their decisions, their emotions, their will, their addiction, and their finances. This is known as codependency, and it hits home with me mostly because of my past. It is a terribly hard cycle to break. Don't misunderstand as I am not saying that the king was, but how easy is it to slip into that mentality that we can rescue others?

Daniel—he was such a man of faith. He knew he had to obey the laws of God, and he knew that God would rescue him. Daniel was able to see past the consequences and his circumstances.

This checked my faith as I questioned myself, "Would I be able to worship under threat of death or a lion's den?" This is something to ponder, and for you to answer. I think, in this country, we take for granted our freedom to worship.

It also strikes me because the king gave Daniel so much favor as it says earlier in the chapter, so why not just write another edict? Because it was the law! How many times do we break God's law and want Him to rescue us and save us from the consequences of our choices, our free will?

> Then the men went as a group to the king and said to him, "Remember, O king, that according to the law of the Medes and Persians no decree or edict that the king issues can be changed." So the king gave the order, and they brought Daniel and threw him into the lions' den. The king said to Daniel, "May your God, whom you serve continually, rescue you!" A stone was brought and placed over the mouth of the den, and the king sealed it with his own signet ring and with the rings of his nobles, so that Daniel's situation might not be changed. (Daniel 6:15-17, NIV)

I like what the king said of Daniel, that he served his God continually, selah . . . Do you serve God continually, truly let yourself be available to serve? Do you acknowledge Him in all your ways? Do you love Him with your whole heart, your whole mind, your whole soul?

One of the ways that we can show our love for God is by our actions, adhering to God's law and taking personal responsibility for our behavior. We cannot save others nor can we save ourselves! My Jehovah Shammah is the God who is there. He is the only one who can rescue us!

Aristotle's Nicomachean Ethics

The theory, written in 350 BC by Aristotle, in its simplest form says that pleasure drives out pain. One of the tenets is that it is because of excessive pain that people pursue excessive pleasure as a cure for their suffering. When I read this little gem, it really struck a chord.

It described my entire life before God. I pursued excessive pleasure to try to block out some of the most excruciatingly painful experiences of my life. My personal struggle with excesses continues despite finally finding the Balm of Gilead, the only cure for every pain we suffer.

Just tonight, at choir practice, I was recounting how far God has brought me. I was telling an old college story about drinking a bottle of whiskey like it was water and seeing three moons that night at one of the many parties in our apartment. I was trying to cure my suffering for years. It lasted well beyond the college party scene and far into my adult life.

Solomon called the pursuit of worldly pleasures "chasing the wind." He came to realize that all the pleasures this world has to offer are empty without God. I was, prior to January 2005, a professional wind chaser.

Biblically speaking, Aristotle's premise is flawed though he described what I believe to be the root of all addictive behaviors: seeking to fill that void that only God can fill and to kill the pain that only God can relieve. I propose that pleasure will not drive out pain. It may dull your senses and distract you from it, but it is not a cure.

Even from a nursing perspective, there are so many physical pain theories and theories about how pain really works in our brains and neurotransmitters and how it should be treated. All the theories and suppositions don't really matter in the end.

Pain is perception, and perception can become reality.

Whether it is physical, emotional, or spiritual pain that you may be dealing with right now, I pray that all of you would seek solace and freedom from your pain in the only Way, the only Truth, and through the only One who can cure you from whatever it is.

There is nothing that He cannot be to you and for you. Isaiah talks about how God can provide the comfort of a mother and how He is our husband, our *Ish*. He is our Abba Father, and our Jehovah Rophe, the Healer and Great Physician. He is Jehovah Jireh, my provider, and my Rock—Jehovah Tsuri. He is my Shepherd, my Jehovah Roi, and my Jehovah Shalom. He can be your joy and your strength if you will only call out to Him and rest upon Him. He will be a consuming fire if you let Him!

There is nothing that Jesus did not go through here on this Earth: He was rejected by his own people—by the very people He came to save. He was tempted. He lived in an earthly tent and knew hunger and thirst. He sang. He knew what it was to be betrayed by a friend, betrayed by a kiss, and He knew what it is to be sold out for some silver. He only went back to Nazareth once. He told his apostles to shake off the dust. He knew! He knows! So whatever it is, *He* can be the Balm of Gilead, and He can mend your wounds no matter what they are from. He can define and change your reality and your perception if you let Him.

For years, I thought my excessive pleasures would cure my pain, but they did not and left me more miserable and in a deeper, darker place. Now I realize and know that I cannot cure my own pain, but God can. At the same time, I fully admit it is a struggle still to not try to do it on my own, and only by the grace of God that I have not had a drink or cigarette in years, taken any illegal substance, or scarfed down a whole cake with buttercream icing. He alone is able, and what He has done for me, He will do for you!

I encourage you to begin to pray for those who have hurt you and extend the love and mercy to them, which Christ has extended to you.

HIDING: WHAT ARE YOU HIDING IN?

Rescue me from my enemies, O Lord, for I hide myself in you.
—Psalms 143:9, NIV

You are my hiding place; you will protect me from trouble and surround me with songs of deliverance.
—Psalms 32:7, NIV

Since, then you have been raised with Christ, set your hearts on things above, where Christ is seated at the right hand of God. Set your mind on things above, not on earthly things. For you died, and your life is now hidden with Christ in God. When Christ, who is your life appears, then you also will appear with Him in glory.
—Colossians 3:1-4

How can a young man keep his way pure? By living according to your word. I seek You with all my heart; do not let me stray from your commands. I have hidden your word in my heart that I might not sin against You. Praise be to You, O Lord; teach me your decrees. With my lips I recount all the laws that come from your mouth. I rejoice in following your statutes as one rejoices in great riches. I meditate on your precepts and consider your ways. I delight in your decrees; I will not neglect your word.
—Psalms 119:9-16

I used to be really good at hiding myself in lots of stuff. As a nurse, it was easy to hide at holidays with the schedule. As the superdysfunctional party girl I used to be, it was easy to hide in alcohol, relationships, and drugs.

Even after I was saved, I still hid. I would turn to food in those moments of emotional upheaval, disappointment, or anger. Not that this behavior was new by any means, but it was intensified. I could no longer grab a cig or a joint and go puff one down. So I would immerse myself in a vat of butter-slathered popcorn, or a bag of my favorite kettle-cooked chips, as in the whole bag with the whole container of the dip. Sometimes, it was fast-food delights filled with that orange cheese that tastes so good or maybe a small wheel of Brie or some other unhealthy culinary concoction to avoid dealing with the "things" of life. Instead of ingesting whatever was being passed around and dancing all night, my drug was the food.

I, literally, was continuing the cycle of stuffing down the pain except now it was with things that were legal. Gluttony with food, though still a sin, was somehow not as bad in my baby Christian mind.

Then, one day, a kind saint so gently brought it to my attention that eating was really part of one's worship. It seems like an obvious concept to grasp, but I will never forget my reaction to the comment.

I replied with "I know, I pray about it everyday," which now brings me to a fit of laughter because it seems like such an absurd comment. However, at the time, I was completely serious and had no clue. It was like saying, "My car is black, and I'm praying for it to be white everyday." It really makes me laugh now, but I was in such a sad place and had no idea.

So God, in His patience and by His Spirit, began to reveal to me that action was required, not just prayer. Furthermore, my prayers, at the time, were not really centered around the root of the issue either, but slowly God has been working that out of me as well. I was repeating the same pattern and bearing the same fruit with self-destructive unhealthy behavior because the root had not been completely plucked out of my heart.

One way God is getting to the root of it all is through the songs He is blessing me with. They uncover bits of pain and then come pouring out of me. He truly has surrounded me with songs of deliverance just like what David talked about. Can you hear Him sing over you? He is. Are you allowing God to get to the root of your pain? He is a very personal and relational God and wants to lavish you with His love and healing.

It is still a constant battle for me everyday. Some days, I lose, but that is because of my own sinful free will. Some days, I submit and allow God His victory.

I do still pray about my food issues as we are commanded to pray without ceasing, but I know that there is another step in the process. Now I take action and do seek to hide myself in His Word for, in *His* Word, we find the only weapon we really need for combat. Wield that double-edged sword in your own battles today!

ANOTHER WORLD

Out my back window, there exists another world. It often looks like something out of a fairy tale.

The other day, there was a chipmunk eating his way toward a rabbit as the birds above them flittered around the neighbor's feeder. The little creatures feeding upon the grass looked like they were going to bump noses, too busy feasting to be concerned about anything else. The woodpeckers and chickadees flew in and out of the shrubs, up to the tree, and back down to the ground. The morning doves walked around, bobbing their heads like they were the cool kids on the block. The blue jays swooped in, and most of the other birds left for a few minutes. In the past, I have seen a mother sparrow giving food to her little fluffy one.

At any given daylight moment, the scene out back looks unreal sometimes. The little creatures look like they should start singing and break into a chorus of some happy song. My cats sit here and stare, making their little noises, like they are so excited and ready to pounce on any of those darling animals God has placed within their view.

Only the window separates them and keeps the peace that exists on both sides of the window. The window prevents chaos. Only God can be the window in my life, preventing my would-be chaos if left to my own devices.

I could open the back door, and the scene could turn into a nasty, blood-filled horror flick real quick. The cats would love the thrill of the chase, the hunt for pleasure! Solomon called that chasing the wind, which simply is the endless pursuit of what the world has to offer and its ultimate emptiness.

I could also open the window but close the screens to let the cats smell the scent of their would-be prey. Temptations are like the screens, aren't they? They make the scene fuzzy, cloud your view, and take away some of the clarity of God's plan for our lives.

Dealing with temptation is not an easy thing as we are all human with wants, desires, and needs. Sometimes, you may have to separate yourself from "it."

> Flee the evil desires of youth, and pursue righteousness, faith, love and peace, along with those who call on the Lord out of a pure heart. (2 Timothy 2:22, NIV)

> And though she spoke to Joseph day after day, he refused to go to bed with her or even be with her. One day he went into the house to attend to his duties, and none of the household servants was inside. She caught him by his cloak and said, "Come to bed with me!" But he left his cloak in her hand and ran out of the house. When she saw that he had left his cloak in her hand and had run out of the house, she called her household servants. "Look," she said to them, "this Hebrew has been brought to us to make sport of us! He came in here to sleep with me, but I screamed. When he heard me scream for help, he left his cloak beside me and ran out of the house." (Genesis 39:10-15, NIV)

We can be attacked when and where we are weakest. Jesus, when he was in the desert, was tempted by a physical need, an emotional need, and a psychological need (see Matthew 4). I believe we can learn from Jesus's response.

First, He used the scripture to fight the attack, but He didn't just quote it. He lived it! He was the Word! He also exerted His spiritual authority and commanded the devil, "Away from me!"

What you want may look good. It could be things you want like a TV, a car, or a new house. It could be people that catch your eye, like the hot iron-pumping Prince Charming or the scantily clad model at the gym. You have to fill in your own blank and know what may be a temptation for you. Self-awareness is the first step, and knowing what your temptations are will help you fight the battle.

What are your current desires that may look appealing but may not be the best thing for you? Sin normally does appear *so* very attractive.

> When the woman saw that the fruit of the tree was good for food and pleasing to the eye, and also desirable for gaining wisdom, she took some and ate it. She also gave some to her husband, who was with her, and he ate it. (Genesis 3:6, NIV)

We all know how that one turned out. The fifteenth verse in Romans seven is so true: "I do not understand what I do. For what I want to do I do not do, but what I hate I do." So how do we deal with it?

The answer is found in the Bible. James 4:1-3 says we basically need to submit ourselves to God. Verse 1 starts off, "What causes fights and quarrels among you? Don't they come from your desires that battle within you?" Sound familiar?

Verse 2 says, "You want something but don't get it. You kill and covet, but you cannot have what you want. You quarrel and fight. You do not have, because you do not ask God." Verse 3 applies very much to our pleasure-driven culture: "When you ask, you do not receive, because you ask with wrong motives, that you may spend what you get on your pleasures."

Maybe, instead of focusing on what you want, it is a better thing to delve into and explore your motives for wanting "it" in the first place and take that issue to God. There may be something deeper behind your desire that only God can heal.

I encourage all of you to walk in the spiritual authority that you have "because the One who is in you is greater than the one who is in the world" (see 1 John 4:4). I also encourage you to feed upon the Word everyday. Jesus commanded us to do so in His rebuke of Satan's temptation, when He quoted Deuteronomy 8:3 ". . . man does not live on bread alone but on every word that comes from the mouth of God." Do you know what *He* says? Let God be the window in your life.

God's Deliverance and the Company Picnic

Last Friday was the corporate America company picnic. It is normally a time for fellowship, food, and fun, or so I thought it would be before I got there.

I was there maybe an hour before I realized just how many times I was asked if I wanted to have a drink. There were bottles all around, clanking within inches of my face. There were peach wine coolers to my right, hard tea directly across the table, beer and white wine to my left. It was like being at a bar or at the club again.

I kept getting the smell of it, especially the wine. Oh! How I used to love white wine (a good Australian blend), expensive champagne (there really is a difference), Cosmopolitans, whiskey sours, dirty martinis, a nice cool beer on a hot day with lime, a good mojito, mint juleps for the big day of horse racing in May, vodka, Spanish fire water . . . The list could go on and on.

I used to love to drink and party. I loved the tastes, the smell, the feeling, and the glass in your hand. I used to *be* the life of the party, and those who knew me back then, I'm sure would agree.

I never knew I had a drinking problem until I stopped. It was not the typical type of problem per se but the "can't just have one" kind of problem and the "can't feel comfortable around a lot of people without a drink" kind of problem. I used alcohol to cope with my insecurities.

Coworkers, whom I consider friends, really had no idea of my struggle. I found myself grabbing at my cross that hung around my neck as I watched what felt like everyone around me drinking.

Then my mind raced to last Christmas when a friend's little girl asked me why I always wear a cross, and I explained it to her so a six year old could understand. I told her the cross that hung around my neck was a reminder of how Jesus died for me personally and my sins just like He died for her and her sins as well. I asked her a few weeks later if she knew why I wore my cross. She repeated my answer to her verbatim. She remembered.

One of the teenagers in our church and in my small singing group also asked me the same question a few weeks ago. She got the more in-depth answer that a teenager could understand with explanations on the importance of realizing that our salvation is personal.

It struck me that the cross around my neck was noticeable to everyone in the outside world. It occurred to me that all the people that see me everyday probably also take notice as well, not just people from the church.

I held my cross in my hand as I walked to my car to leave the company picnic, thanking God for His deliverance. I remember all the times I used to drink until quite drunk and how God kept me safe. It is only because of God that I am still alive at all—by His strength, His grace, His mercy, His love, and His Spirit.

I do, normally, wear a cross everyday. For me, the cross I wear is more than just a piece of jewelry that hangs from my neck just like I told my friend's little girl. It is a tangible reminder of how Jesus died for me, how much He loves me, and even how He loved me in the midst all of my sin—of which there was more than an abundance of. It is a reminder of how He sacrificed Himself, how He pursued me, and how He cares for me. It is a physical reminder that I never want to knowingly or purposefully disrespect the gift that was so freely given with my thoughts or actions.

The Bible says, in Matthew 5, that we are the salt and the light. I will let my light shine, for I am not ashamed. What can you do today to let His light shine through you and your life?

That cross means something so real to me, and I want to shout about what God has done for me from the mountaintops, but I know my actions will speak louder than anything that comes out of my mouth. What do your actions say about what you believe?

He is real, His love is real, and His salvation is real. I will praise Him everyday for that.

Matthew 10:38 says, "And anyone who does not take his cross and follow me is not worthy of me." Everyone has a different cross to bear and a different unique story to tell. What is yours?

Matthew 16:24 reads, "Then Jesus said to his disciples, 'If anyone would come after me, he must deny himself and take up his cross and follow me.'" Luke 9:23 says, "Then he said to them all: 'If anyone would come after me, he must deny himself and take up his cross daily and follow me.'" These two are basically the same verse, but it is worth noting that, in Luke, he notes that Jesus said we must take our cross up daily. It is a daily process, denying of ourselves and our will and submitting to the change.

Having canceled the written code, with its regulations, that was against us and that stood opposed to us; he took it away, nailing it to the cross. And having disarmed the powers and authorities, he made a public spectacle of them, triumphing over them by the cross. (Colossians 2:14-15)

For we know that our old self was crucified with Him so that the body of sin might be done away with, that we should no longer be slaves to sin. (Romans 6:6)

Are you ready to be a slave to righteousness today? What sin have you been a slave to? God's deliverance is available for all.

You Asked and You Said

(This devotional was my response to an e-mail I received.)

Question No. 1. You asked about scripture being warped by different folks, and how do you tell the difference?

I too have read things, or heard things, and thought to myself, *That scripture doesn't mean that at all.* My initial reaction to your question is that you need to use discernment when listening to others' teachings while guarding your eyes and ears. Not everyone on TV or everyone who proclaims to be a Christian really is. Evil comes to church too. The enemy knows the Word. Remember the powers and principalities and all that we fight against. The Word says there will be those who will tickle your ears as well.

Second Timothy 4:3 reads, "For the time will come when men will not put up with sound doctrine. Instead, to suit their own desires, they will gather around them a great number of teachers to say what their itching ears want to hear." First Timothy 4:1 says, "The Spirit clearly says that in later times some will abandon the faith and follow deceiving spirits and things taught by demons."

I will tell you that I do not watch TV and do not have cable. God dealt with me regarding this issue because I had made it an idol, and even when I got saved, I was watching more Christian TV than actually spending time in the Word. God spoke to my spirit and said, "Do you want to know what they say or what I say?" I would encourage you to turn off the tube and just spend your own time in the Word and let God speak to you through it.

God's Word is alive, and I believe the more time you spend with God, in the Word, the more real He becomes. I believe that the Holy Spirit is our counselor, and I believe that the Holy Spirit will "check" you if something is not right. I have felt this "check" myself and know if someone is using scripture and putting their spin on it to manipulate the situation.

My other thought is that Satan himself is the author of confusion. God does not want you to be confused, least of all by His holy Word.

Question No. 2. You said that you are being told so many "different ways" to be "a Christian."

My initial reaction to this is that there really is only one way, and that is to acknowledge

1. that Christ died for your sins;
2. that you accept Jesus into your heart;
3. that you recognize the Bible is the Word of God; and
4. that God exists as the Father, the Son, and the Holy Spirit.

The concept of religion is the reason why most people on this earth despise church, hate religious Holy Rollers, and think horrible things about God. If you *are* in a right relationship with God, everything else falls into place, and you become more and more like Christ. Christianity needs to be about relationship, not religion and someone else's definition of what being a Christian means. God, through His holy Word, defines that.

People will know you by your fruit and see who you are. Your actions will speak louder than words.

The works and fruit naturally flow out of your being in that right relationship automatically, but there is nothing that you can "do" to make Him love you more once you lay it all at the foot of the cross. However, there is a process, and it is called sanctification. Usually this takes time and is a process, and we are all in this process no matter where we are in our walk. Until the day we die, we are being made into the image of Christ.

People will often quote James 2:26 (KJV) saying "Faith without works is dead." What I believe God was trying to say was that "the acting out of your faith and love for your Father is necessary and is displayed by your behavior." In real life, this means that you show your faith everyday just by your existence, just by being in that right relationship. The light of Christ will shine through you in all situations.

God will grant you wisdom; you just need to ask. That is biblical, and it is in James (chapter 1:5-8, NIV):

> If any of you lacks wisdom, he should ask God, who gives generously to all without finding fault, and it will be given to him. But when he asks, he must believe and not doubt, because he who doubts is like a wave of the sea, blown and tossed by the wind. That man should not think he will receive anything from the Lord; he is a double-minded man, unstable in all he does.

Question No. 3. You said, in your prayer conversation with God, that He was saying, "This is how you can show me you trust me."

If God has given you specific ways, then you need to be obedient, using wisdom and His strength. I too had a "Do you trust Me" moment with God. I was being worked up for the gastric bypass and really seeking God's face and His will on the matter. I was praying, and that small still voice asked, "Do you trust Me?" So needless to say, I never got the surgery. I have lost thirty pounds over ten months. It has been gradual, but I was obedient, and I believe our obedience honors God.

God has a purpose and plan for all of us. Jeremiah 29:11-14 reads, "'For I know the plans I have for you,' declares the Lord, 'plans to prosper you and not to harm you, plans to give you hope and a future. Then you will call upon me and come and pray to me, and I will listen to you. You will seek me and find me when you seek me with all your heart.' 'I will be found by you,' declares the Lord, 'and will bring you back from captivity . . .'"

We need to seek Him will all of our heart. We need to pray, and He will listen. He is there for the finding. It requires a decision and action on our part to be in His will.

Question No. 4. You asked, "All I have to do is change my thinking and try to bite my tongue, right?"

I believe that the process of sanctification changes your thinking so you won't have to bite your tongue. I believe that the Holy Spirit takes up residence within us and changes our thinking. God touches our hearts and changes us so that we may exert the self-discipline or self-control (sound mind) that He has given us. Second Timothy 1:7 says, "For God did not give us a spirit of timidity, but a spirit of power, of love and of self-discipline."

I would encourage you to walk in that power. Know who you are in Him. If you don't know what and who He says you are, then ask and He will show you.

There is also a process of justification, which is the process of being made right with God. Titus 3:4-7 deals with both sanctification and justification:

> But when the kindness and love of God our Savior appeared, he saved us, not because of righteous things we had done, but because of his mercy. He saved us through the washing of rebirth and renewal by the Holy Spirit, whom he poured out on us generously through Jesus Christ our Savior, so that, having been justified by his grace, we might become heirs having the hope of eternal life.

I encourage you to seek, love, and simply be with Him through prayer, in silence, in His Word, and in all things. Only He can save us from ourselves!

Search, Cleanse, and Heal

I Need to Feel Your Love Divine

LIBERTY AND FREEDOM

Please read Galatians 5-6.

Section I

Today was my wedding anniversary three years ago. We were married several months before the Lord brought me back to Him. It was a beautiful October day at the museum, by the bench where we would sit and talk for hours when we were dating. We exchanged vows and exchanged rings.

The retired pastor, his wife, the ducks, and some passersby were the only ones in attendance. It was a day of mixed emotions, and though the pictures are filled with smiling faces, there is a deep sadness behind my eyes. Things did not go as planned. I was not able to wear the beautiful gown that hung in my closet for several years after that fateful day.

One night, several weeks before our planned, low-budget nuptials, while I was sleeping, the phone rang. Startled and bit shaky, I picked up the phone. A nurse calmly announced who she was and where she was calling from. She told me my fiancé had been stabbed. I began arguing with her and asking if he was dead and assuring her that I was a nurse, and she could tell me the truth. She insistently told me that I needed to come to the emergency room.

When I arrived, I found my other car pulled up to the emergency room entrance with the driver's door wide open. I suppose, when you are the victim of a violent crime, parking the car is not a priority. I was honestly scared at that point and truly thought he was dead.

I walked in and nervously asked where he was. They took me back to his bed. I walked in to find him sitting up and awake. It was a relief and a joyous moment.

He was to have been at work that night, but I could smell alcohol on his breath. When I asked him about that, he told me to give him a breath mint.

Without thinking, I did and then listened to his explanation that he and a friend were in the parking lot at work, and that he only had a small amount of alcohol. He began recounting the events and details that led to this moment in time. Slowly my joy that he was alive became confusion intertwined with dizzying unbelief and doubtful angst.

The police came in to take his statement right there in the emergency room. I listened, hanging on every word, to see if it made sense. I thought maybe I was just tired and confused since it was the middle of the night. His story did make sense at the time in part. The officer told him he would need to contact the detectives downtown to answer additional questions at a later date.

His wounds healed quickly as the blade narrowly missed his lungs and vital vessels that run along the top part of the chest. His shoulder did not seem to be affected, and the cut on his face closed very fast. It seemed as if this freak act of violence would soon be behind us. We had enough to deal with.

Section II

I had just lost our baby with my pregnancy ending at ten and a half weeks, only several days prior to the stabbing. I was recovering from the procedure that they had to perform as the baby's heart had stopped beating and I was not miscarrying.

I even waited an extra week before having the procedure done, hoping that the dates were just wrong and that, at the next check, we would see that little thumping on the ultrasound screen. But it was not to be. There was no thump, and there was no growth.

I remember that things were somewhat tense between us. He had left me alone that night after the procedure, supposedly, to go out with friends. I was too impaired from the anesthesia to really put up a fuss.

His behavior, once we found out that the baby's heart was not beating, was somewhat surprising. It did not make sense. After all, we were pregnant on purpose, and both agreed that we wanted to have a child together and were planning on getting married that next month. We did not need this added drama of the stabbing.

He went to speak with the detectives the week after the stabbing, and all seemed to be getting back to normal. Even though my heart was breaking, and my life seemed to be crumbling apart piece by piece, the wedding was a happy thing for us to focus on at the time.

A day or so after his meeting with the detectives, his grandmother called highly upset with him. I could hear her yelling through the phone. He began vehemently defending himself. Apparently, the news had hit the local paper of his "alleged story" to the detectives, which included another woman.

After the call from his grandmother, he shared with me that the detectives had warned him that he was in violation of his parole since he was out that night and not at work like he was supposed to be. He weaved a tale that made it seem as if the rest of the world was against us, even threatening to sue the paper for lying about his statements to the detectives, and that there was no other woman.

We were both scared that the police were going to come and take him away at any time. Out of fear, we were married at the end of that month, moving the date up by a week or so, before any additional legal action could occur. I had to go to work that night and cried on and off most of the way through the shift. I had tried calling him several times to no avail, and with every call that was not answered, my heart shattered into a million pieces.

I was so embarrassed by the situation that I didn't tell anyone about the marriage until very early the next morning toward the end of the shift. The girls I worked with, bless their hearts, had a shower for me a week or so later for which I was so appreciative.

It would not be until two months after our marriage at the museum that he would be taken away from me in cuffs after the hearing. I was devastated to say the least.

I hated the lead detective, with a fiery passion, and blamed him for twisting the evidence in their favor. I was so lost, lonely, and felt that the world was against me. I was completely broken.

I raced home to wait for his call. I knew he would be allowed to make one call, and it would be to me, his loving wife who had carried his child for a brief time.

Section III

Two days went by, and there was no call. I was confused and ready to just lie in a curled-up ball and never face the world again or set foot out of my front door.

Eventually, I mustered enough energy to go down to my car, which he had driven. There, on the front seat, were homemade documents in different stages of creation supposedly from the Register of Wills office. The body of the letter said something to the effect:

Dear Mr. So-and-So,

This letter is in response to your request for verification that this office has no record that you have ever been married.

My mind flashed back to one night several weeks prior. We were watching TV, and he had gotten out all the papers for our marriage license application. I wasn't really paying attention to what he was doing at the time, but hindsight made it perfectly clear.

My mind then came to the present, back to this moment in time, as the tears began to well up in my eyes. My mind started to race. I then pulled paper after paper off the front seat in a flurry. One paper after the next, my eyes scanned faster and faster. Some had the local county seal; some had typos in the body. The print was becoming blurred through the tears that began streaming down my face.

Then, hidden and tucked in between the seat and the middle consul, I found the letter. It was addressed to a woman. I could not believe my eyes. The letter even had a stamp on it. It was ready and waiting to be mailed.

Looking back, I believe he honestly thought that he would not be locked up again and would win at the trial. I had spent a decent amount of money and retained an expensive attorney who, in the end, was no help at all.

At any rate, I took the letter into the house, and slowly opened it. It was like time was suspended, and nothing was real. It was basically a love letter. As I came to the end of it, where he expressed his feelings for her, I began crying in such a way that bordered on screaming—the heart-and-soul, gut-wrenching cry of grief and pain.

Then, in a momentary break from crying, I used all the tactics I knew to try and locate a phone number, but it did not seem to be listed. I then opened my phone bill that had been sitting there unopened . . . and there was a long-distance number dialed over and over again. My heart sank even further especially when I noted the dates.

I dialed it without really pondering what I would say. She answered. I introduced myself as his wife through my tears. She was stunned and was not really sure what to say. She was also in a state of disbelief.

Eventually, she told me that one of his friends that he introduced her to, A, was a bartender at a local restaurant and thought that maybe this friend of his could help piece together more parts of the puzzle. I went with some friends the next day and found this friend of his to tell her I was his wife and try to get information from her. The conversation went something like this:

"Are you so-and-so, a friend of Mr. thus-and-such?"

She said, "Yes, can I help you?"

I replied, "My name is Mrs. S, and I am his wife, but I guess I'm not the wife you were introduced to."

Her jaw dropped, and her eyes widened like saucers. She was shocked and initially speechless. When she regained her composure, she told me that he introduced another girl as his wife to her and all of their mutual friends. I told her I knew, and that I had been in contact with the other woman and was on my way to meet her.

I left the restaurant with more questions and no real answers. A, his friend, really did not have any more pieces of truth for me, only more lies that he had told. I then made the lonely drive to the diner to meet the other woman who shared not only my first name, but who also shared a life with my husband.

Section IV

She was pretty and very nice to me. She had two of her own businesses, and she was a smart girl. He apparently was in a very serious relationship with this other woman as they were also planning on having a child. She wanted to see the wedding pictures, so I showed them to her. She said that she had no idea he was married. I believed her.

I eventually found out that he spent our wedding night with her while I cried my way through work that night. I shared the early baby ultrasound pictures with her. I pulled out my marriage certificate. I kept showing her the things of our life together, item after item, as it was all proof of his falling house of cards.

She told me the whole story of their relationship. He was with her the night after my pregnancy ended, and that was the night they began "dating." She was heartbroken when she learned this and was apologetic.

He was traveling down to see her frequently as she lived in the next town. He told her that the girl always talking in the background while they were on the phone was his sister. He had been talking to her on the phone the whole time right in front of me. When he brought her to my house with bills lying around in my name, she did not really question it because I was supposedly dead.

He had told her and all of her friends that Julie Petrie was dead and had been a former family friend so close to them that I had left the house to his family after my passing. I honestly believe he may have been seeking to do me harm. Why else would he have told people that I was dead? I believe now that his incarceration was God's protection covering me.

Not only had he lied to the police about the night of his stabbing, lied to his friend and to the other woman about our marriage, lied about my supposed demise and passing while cheating on me the entire time, but I would also soon discover that his whole life was a lie. I began talking to his family and asking many questions about everything he ever told me. He never even served in the military as he said he did. Everything, absolutely everything he had ever told me, was a lie.

I was blind to his deceit. The betrayal I felt was indescribable. This was way more intense than dealing with a moment of infidelity.

There was a complete breakdown of my whole world and everything I had built my life around. I was seeking to fill the void in my broken heart from the pain of my youth, the abandonment by my parents, and the years of every type of abuse imaginable at the hands of those who were supposed to have loved and protected me. I wanted a family and children of my very own so I could do it right. I wanted to experience unconditional love and thought that having a child and getting married would surely be the answer I was so desperately in search of. My short pregnancy and my marriage changed nothing. I wanted to die and was ready to give up on life yet once again.

It was not until about a month later that I found a reason to live. I ended up at the altar, rededicating my life to Christ after a friend, who would become my spiritual mother, invited me to her church. The prodigal daughter had finally returned home!

Section V

It was three years ago today, that I followed my flesh into bondage, before I ever really remembered anything about the Spirit or knew anything about the freedom that only Christ can bring.

Today is a strange day. I am still dealing with the consequences of my former life, before my rebirth in Christ, mostly in terms of finances, but today, it seems to be more in terms of my emotions.

It is funny that, yesterday, I couldn't even remember if we got married on the twenty-sixth or the twenty-eighth, but today, I am quite sure. The stranger thing is that it seems like it was so long ago, almost like it all happened in a dream.

I found myself recently telling someone how disobedience comes at a cost. In my former life, being out of God's will came at a very high cost, figuratively and literally, just as obedience now in my walk comes at a price. Having to die to this flesh everyday is not such an easy thing.

Some days, I get so caught up in all the things I am still doing wrong, and then somehow I begin to look in the rear view mirror. This brings into focus the horrible, sinful things I have done in my past. That is bondage and it is an evil scheme of the enemy.

I'm sure you can imagine the tears as I read the first verse in Galatians 5: "It is for freedom that Christ has set us free. Stand firm, then, and do not let yourselves be burdened again by a yoke of slavery." God has a way of sending reminders right on time and today I needed to read those very words and hear the voice of God telling me that I am free. My past is forgotten and my sin is forgiven.

The Jewish people had their law like in the Galatians reading. For them, their law and tradition was their life. It was not just their religion; it was their very culture and character. The whole mess that Paul was dealing with was over circumcision but replace that with anything in your life that is keeping you in bondage, and it applies to all of us in our everyday life.

Paul tells them that they have fallen from grace because they are focusing on the law. They are trying to make themselves right by following the letter of the law. It is a reminder that it is only God's grace, freely given, that makes us right, and it is only Christ who makes us free.

A friend recently passed along Romans 5:9-11 which says,

> Since we have now been justified by His blood, how much more shall we be saved from God's wrath through Him! For if, when we were God's enemies, we were reconciled to Him through the death of His Son, how much more having been reconciled, shall we be saved through His Life! Not only is this so, but we also rejoice in God through our Lord Jesus Christ, through whom we now received reconciliation.

Reconciliation and justification are through Christ and Christ alone. It is not just by my repentance or anything I can do, and it is not by being in bondage over stuff from my past and feeling bad about it. It is not by the law but only through Christ: through His blood, His death, His sacrifice, and His resurrection.

My prayer for all of you is that you walk in the freedom and grace which God has given you, and that none of you are entangled in a yoke of bondage but know that His yoke is light and His burden is easy! Amen! Let your anthem of freedom through Christ ring today!

JEHOVAH TSIDQENU

"The days are coming," declares the LORD, "when I will raise up to David a righteous Branch, a King who will reign wisely and do what is just and right in the land. In his days Judah will be saved, and Israel will live in safety. This is the name by which he will be called: *The Lord Our Righteousness.*"

—Jeremiah 23:5-6, NIV

Yahweh (or Jehovah) Tsidqenu (pronounced tSid-k-new) is the Hebrew name for *The Lord Our Righteousness*. I had this total "God moment" the other day while writing to a dear friend when God revealed another part of Himself. The e-mail went like this:

This is not about me, but about Him, and the total submission, the total surrender to Him: to really let my life be a living sacrifice, to really turn it all over to Him, to be in right relationship with Him, and to be restored to His likeness.

That is how God revealed Himself to me as the Lord My Righteousness.

What does that mean? I believe it is simply God working through us, making us right, and bringing us into the right relationship with Him so that we truly reflect Him. God speaks "rightness" into my life and "rightness" into my spirit.

Righteousness cannot be just about our behavior that is outwardly expressed obviously, or that would just be legalism. What about all the stuff that we hang on to inside? What about the wrongness in us and the inability to let "it" all go?

We all have things that we need to let go of. We all have the "*it*" in our lives that hinders our righteousness. I love the saying "Let go and let God." That makes it sound so easy.

—

Why is the reality of letting "it" all go and surrendering "it" all to Him such a hard thing to actually do, submitting to the process of being restored into His likeness and His rightness (besides the fact that we are stuck in this flesh)? Maybe the answer is in Romans 3:10, which reads, "There is no one righteous, not even one." Continue down into verse 20 where it says, "No one will be declared righteous by observing the law . . ." Verse 23 and 24 says, "For all have sinned and fall short of the glory of God and are justified freely by His grace through the redemption that came by Christ Jesus."

I believe Paul was trying to say that righteousness is not something that you do but something that you are, that it is a state of being—being in that relationship with Jehovah Tsidqenu and believing in that justification that was freely given by His grace through Jesus.

So it can't be about the action of me somehow letting "it" all go, or my decision to surrender "it" all, because that would be me trying to do something once again instead of just being in that right relationship. I need to let God work out the details, work out the past once and for all.

So I think, in my "God moment" above, the part that was most true in my revelation was that my Jehovah Tsidqenu is more interested in me being in a right relationship with Him, being restored to His likeness, and my life being a living sacrifice unto Him. It is the realization and true recognition that I can do nothing by myself about the "it" that needs to be gotten rid of within me. He will root it out if I quit trying to *do* it and just *be*.

I pray that you are all encouraged about the "it" in your own lives, that you are able to just *be*, and that Jehovah Tsidqenu will reveal Himself in your life.

The Lord is righteous in *all* His ways . . . (Psalms 145:17)

"I am the vine, you are the branches. If a man remains in Me, and I in him, he will bear much fruit; apart from Me, you can do nothing. (John 15:5)

STILL IN THE PEEL-AND-HEAL PROCESS

Show proper respect to everyone: Love the brotherhood of believers, fear God, honor the king.

—1 Peter 2:17

A gentle answer turns away wrath, but a harsh word stirs up anger.

—Proverbs 15:1

Get rid of all bitterness, rage and anger, brawling and slander, along with every form of malice. Be kind and compassionate to one another, forgiving each other, just as in Christ, God forgave you.

—Ephesians 4:31-32

Me and my big mouth is where the problem started, but where it ended was an entirely different place. Of course, the apology to God was first for the way I had treated one of His children (again), followed by the apology to that particular child of God (again), and followed by some serious reflection and prayer (again—argh!). This most recent little outburst was not the first, and I'm sure not the last. As I began to really try to figure out why the pattern kept repeating, God started to reveal this self-loathing part of me, which was hindering my ability to fully accept others.

The tears came along with the realization that there are still some things that I have desperately been trying to let go of without really ever accepting them first. I never really said "God, my name is Julie, and I have some issues" and then proceed to name them all. Maybe I need to.

Recently, a coworker caught me looking at myself in the mirror as I was putting on lipstick. It was more than just looking at my lips because I was actually examining my face and what was looking back at me. She laughed and said "Oh, you are beautiful," and in a moment of vulnerability, I said "Really?" as I tried not to cry. It was a strange moment in corporate America, and I just wanted to run to my car and pour out my guts to God about why I don't feel pretty and all the mess behind my low self-esteem.

So I told a fellow believer about this lipstick moment, and I was called out. She said, "You were looking because you really think you are ugly and were trying to cover it up." Ouch!

It is hard to accept who you are sometimes on the inside and outside. It can be difficult to be so transparent to the world without feeling like you have to cover it up.

However, that is the beauty of having a relationship with God. You never have to hide anything. He will love you in spite of yourself and love you regardless of anything you may think about who you are, whether it is in a moment of insecurity or a whole lifetime full of it. The other beautiful thing is that He will reveal who He has made you to be if you will let Him and if you will listen to His small, still voice.

This lipstick incident took me back to my mouth and the ugliness within me that I have been trying to get rid of without acknowledging the root of the issue or accepting it first. The layers of mine, covering up the ugliness, are starting to be peeled back. I am still in the process of allowing God to peel and then heal.

> But God demonstrates his own love for us in this: While we were still sinners, Christ died for us. (Romans 5:8)

> Accept one another, then, just as Christ accepted you, in order to bring praise to God. (Romans 15:7)

For anyone who deals with low self-esteem, self-loathing, or self-doubt, I pray you let Romans 15:7 speak to your heart and let God teach you how to love yourself and really accept who you are in Him. Often times, we are the only thing holding ourselves back.

GUILT FREE

Let us draw near to God with a sincere heart in full assurance of faith, having our hearts sprinkled to cleanse us from a guilty conscience and having our bodies washed with pure water.
—Hebrews 10:22, NIV

So often, we have trouble receiving God's mercy and forgiveness. I thought of my own struggle with regard to this issue and found this scripture. How hard is it to believe that you really are forgiven and believe that there is no need for guilt and shame? This is a tough concept for me to really grasp and to let sink deeply into my heart.

From sixth grade on, I was in Catholic schools, going to mass every Sunday and then usually once a week during school hours. I remembered, the other day, that I was one of the cantors, a worship leader in essence, during high school. I found a picture of me at my baccalaureate mass, the night before high school graduation, where my hand was raised to cue everyone to sing, but I also remember that, to me, it wasn't worship. It was more like . . . just singing. It was not drawing near to God for me like it is now.

I think back on those years of believing that Jesus was the Son of God, but I never really felt cleansed or forgiven. I was without a relationship with my Maker. I had no idea that you could actually even have a relationship with someone you cannot see.

I believed in Him, but I didn't know Him—really know Him. I had religion throughout my many years of education. I had two or three college-level religion classes as a part of my bachelor's program at a prestigious Catholic college. As a matter of fact, I had religion classes all the way from sixth to twelfth grade too, but there were no classes on relationship and forgiveness. I felt no connection with the Son of God, Son of Man, God the Father, or the Spirit; the Triune and Elohim were nothing more than words on a page to me.

I am not saying that a relationship cannot be found with God through Catholicism. I am simply saying that I did not find Him through religion and can only speak about my personal experience. I have many Catholic friends, coworkers, and family members who feel they can connect with God through Catholicism. I encourage them on their journey.

My journey has taken me in a different direction as I have found a relationship through different means that is more satisfying than any relationship I have ever known. Yet my human mind still cannot comprehend the overwhelming love that God has for a wretched sinner like me. I still can't wrap my head around the forgiveness that is available for all.

Today I make a choice to accept the love and forgiveness for everything I did wrong in life. I will let go of the guilt and shame. The new choice for me is to be guilt free! I will no longer accept the accusations and lies of the enemy that would try to keep me bound up in my own guilt and shame from a past that is no longer remembered by the Almighty, by El Roi (which translates to the God Who Sees Me).

If you look in Genesis 16:13-14, Hagar gave this name to God when He spoke to her. This is the God who knows your past, present, and future—who sees and knows all.

I pray that all of you are able to receive what was freely given and know that you are able to draw close to *Him* and have a relationship with Him. I pray that you choose to live guilt free and nurture that relationship, the most important relationship that you will ever have—the vertical One!

Consequence versus Punishment

My spiritual mother recently asked me what the difference is between suffering a consequence versus being punished. I replied quickly, "Intent!" Though the more I ponder the question, the more I believe there may not really be a difference at all except only in our earthly thinking.

God will allow us to suffer consequences. He will discipline us. Hebrews 12 talks about it in verse 10: ". . . God disciplines us for our good that we may share in His holiness."

The debt that I accrued as a result of my poor choices was not *poofed* away by God. I had to sell my house and a car and I continue to pay the credit card companies. God has used those consequences to teach me about His financial plan and tithing.

There are a few biblical examples of God's punishment that come immediately to mind: Moses not being allowed to enter into the Promised Land, Myriam's punishment for her attitude and resulting leprosy, and the rebellious men led by Korah being swallowed up by the earth. Through those examples, we see that God's punishment is a very real thing.

However, we also see that the intention was to teach and correct not only those individuals but those that surrounded them. We should be grateful that God would care so much about us!

If God by His very nature is love, then it stands that His intention in both punishment and consequence would be love. Remember His ways are not our ways, and His thoughts are not our thoughts.

A Father's Love

As I sat here one Saturday, in my isolation—trying desperately not to think of anything, not to feel anything, and just be in the moment—I found my thoughts racing even faster than normal through my mind. "I gotta do this" and "I have to do that" and "I really need to get ready for this" were all I could hear. The incessant blah blah blah of my internal voice raced on and on!

Then my mind slowed suddenly, and for some reason, I began to remember how sick I was in high school. My mind jumped back to the late '80s, back to Harrisburg. I can remember going to the emergency room of the local hospital with my dad. They knew something was seriously wrong with me, but they didn't know what. Initially, they thought it was meningitis, which is potentially fatal.

At any rate, I remember the flurry of activity in the ER. The doctors were running all sorts of tests and painful procedures like spinal taps, and I remember being a patient for several weeks on the pediatric floor after that night. I would sneak out with my friends into the lounge area to smoke cigarettes. The staff hated me. Not only was I a teen on a pediatric floor, but I also smoked. I can remember lots of things about that time, but what was heavy on my heart was my father's worry and concern for me.

All of a sudden, the tears were pouring out me as I wondered why my own mother could not have felt the same worry and concern. I, immediately, was saying, "God, I don't want to do this—not now. I'm so sick of this, I don't want to cry over my mother anymore, about all the things that led up to my adoption that happened so long ago. I don't want to go there."

But "there" we went together, and in that small, still voice, He spoke to my heart that it doesn't matter what anyone else has or has not felt for me because He has felt all those things and more for me—a love so great that it was unimaginable. So I cried out "Abba, Father," and He answered.

There is something so beautiful in the expression of the Father's love for all of us.

For you did not receive a spirit that makes you a slave again to fear, but you received the Spirit of sonship. And by Him we cry, "Abba, Father." (Romans 8:15)

Because you are sons, God sent the Spirit of his Son into our hearts, the Spirit who calls out, "Abba, Father." (Galatians 4:6)

"Abba, Father," he said, "everything is possible for you. Take this cup from me. Yet not what I will, but what you will." (Mark 14:36)

Now that I have a relationship with Him, Matthew 6:9-13 means so much. It is the words that Jesus taught us to pray, the very words that He spoke to His Father. I would encourage you to really meditate upon the passage, upon its meaning, and let the message be burned into your mind, your heart, and your soul.

This, then, is how you should pray: Our Father in heaven, hallowed be your name, your kingdom come, your will be done on earth as it is in heaven. Give us today our daily bread. Forgive us our debts, as we also have forgiven our debtors. And lead us not into temptation, but deliver us from the evil one.

No matter what it is in your life that you are trying not to think about or whatever it is that is making you say "I don't want to go there," let God take you to that place. Regardless of how others may have treated you, He will be with you, and He loves you more than you could ever imagine.

THE EYES ARE THE WINDOWS
OF THE SOUL

Ahab cast a covetous eye at Naboth's vineyard, David a lustful eye at Bathsheba. The eye is the pulse of the soul; as physicians judge the heart by the pulse, so we by the eye; a rolling eye, a roving heart. The good eye keeps minute time, and strikes when it should; the lustful, crochet-time, and so puts all out of tune.
—Thomas Adams, English clergyman of wit and learning
(fl. 1612-1653)

I need no dictionary of quotations to remind me that the eyes are the windows of the soul.
—Max Beerbohm, English essayist, caricaturist, and parodist
(1872-1956)

The eye is the inlet to the soul, and it is well to beware of him whose visual organs avoid your honest regard.
—Hosea Ballou, American clergyman and founder of Universalism
(1771-1852)

The eye is the lamp of the body. If your eyes are good, your whole body will be full of light.
—Matthew 6:22

It was probably more than a year after my ex-husband left me. I had unhooked my DVD player and hooked up the VCR. When I tried to put a workout video in, it would not let me. I was more than a little surprised that there was already a "movie" in there.

—

The flick quickly got tossed into the trash where it belonged, but it made me ponder not just how the issue of pornography and sexual addiction had impacted my own life and destroyed my marriage, but that the eyes are truly the windows of the soul. What you fill up on, lust or love, and what you let your eyes see can impact your entire life. Seems like a pretty basic concept, but one worth being reminded of.

Without TV, it is easier for me to guard my own eyes, but sex is still everywhere. It seems like our whole culture is sexualized. Every morning, when I drive to work, there is a billboard that says, "Reading's favorite strip joint." It is an advertisement for a local bar, and it shows a picture of a juicy steak. The sexual connotation is obvious.

I once read that the definition of lust was continual taking without giving and that love conversely was all about giving—that lust was selfish, and that love was selfless. In a culture that sends many mixed messages about what love is, I would encourage you to look to Christ as the perfect manifestation of God's love and the perfect example of what love is. He is the only perfect love that any of us can ever really know. If the divine love relationship is on track, all the rest of your relationships will follow, and Christ's love will permeate to those around you.

For those of you who are married, I would encourage you to take a minute and look into the eyes of your spouse without saying anything at all. What do you see? You may be able to see an actual reflection of yourself if you look closely. You should be able to see a reflection of Christ reflected in your marriage and in your lives together. Have you shown your spouse the love of Christ today? Is your divine love relationship on track?

For those who are not married or married to an unsaved spouse or even struggling in your own Christian marriage, Isaiah 54 reminds us that the Lord your maker is your first husband. Jesus is the lover of your soul. Work on the vertical relationship, and all else will fall into place.

Shine

Let Your Living Water Flow

COMMIT AND TRUST

Commit means to pledge oneself to something. The New King James Version says, in Psalms 37:5, "Commit your way to the Lord, Trust also in Him, And He shall bring it to pass."

Have you committed your way to the Lord? What does that mean for you to really commit your way? I believe David was trying to say that we need to pledge ourselves totally to God, in all aspects, with every part of our lives: from the biggest detail to the smallest, from the biggest emotional crisis to the smallest decision, from the mountaintops to the valleys.

To truly turn it *all* over to God is such an amazing act of faith, which is why I believe David then points out that we must trust in Him. It was not long ago that I remember trusting only in myself.

In nursing school, I remember learning about the locus of control. It was a fancy way to say how people view the world. If they feel they are in control of their lives, they have an internal locus of control. If they feel that something controls them and their life, this means they have an external locus of control.

At the time, I was totally living with an internal locus of control. I felt that I had full power over my life, that I could somehow make my own way in this world, and that I could do it on my own.

I had been doing life on my own from very early on. This false sense of security in all my own ways was a protective survival mechanism. I thought I knew best, and I thought I knew what life was really all about.

I thought the people that I had surrounded myself with, my friends and my pseudofamily, would always be there for me, and would never let me down. I had trust in myself, in the world, and in people.

It took an awful lot to break me of my self-trust: my best friend died, my circle of college friends of twelve years abandoned me because of the would-be husband and his incarceration as Auntie JewelsS was not setting a good example, the fiancé before the husband left me, taking his children that I mothered for two years and would not let me see them, leaving me with two cars, a house, and a whole lot of credit card debt. I could go on and on but will stop there. I never knew I was so hardheaded.

So I thank God that He broke me so that He could fix me and put me back together the way I was supposed to be in the first place. Now, my trust is only in God.

> Trust in the Lord with all your heart and lean not on your own understanding; in all your ways acknowledge Him, and He will make your paths straight. (Proverbs 3:5-6, NIV)

The scripture talks about "in all your ways," acknowledge Him. To me, this means giving God the recognition that He has given everything to us: the material things we see with our eyes, our spiritual gifts and talents, our feelings and emotions, our intelligence, our faults, our weaknesses, the stars and all of creation . . . everything! I love how Paul talks about how he can only boast about his weaknesses. In our weakness, He is strong. We can only be strong in *Him*.

It takes courage to have faith. It takes courage to trust. It takes courage to love. It takes courage to have patience. It takes courage to have commitment. Proverbs 16:3 (NKJV) says, "Commit your works to the Lord, And your thoughts will be established." The NIV translation states it this way: "Commit to the Lord whatever you do, and your plans will succeed" (Proverbs 16:3, NIV). First Peter 4:19 (NIV) reads, "So then, those who suffer according to God's will should commit themselves to their faithful Creator and continue to do good."

Jesus's commitment to us can be found in John 10:11-12 (NIV):

> I am the good shepherd. The good shepherd lays down his life for the sheep. The hired hand is not the shepherd who owns the sheep. So when he sees the wolf coming, he abandons the sheep and runs away. Then the wolf attacks the flock and scatters it.

The choices you make reveal your commitment.

> But if serving the Lord seems undesirable to you, then choose for yourselves this day whom you will serve, whether the Gods your forefathers served beyond the River, or the Gods of the Amorites, in whose land you are living. But as for me and my household, we will serve the Lord. (Joshua 24:15, NIV)

My prayer for you is what Paul says in Acts 20:32: "Now I commit you to God and to the word of His grace, which can build you up and give you an inheritance." Will you commit all your ways to God today and trust in Him?

FAITH WITHOUT DEEDS

What good is it, my brothers, if a man claims to have faith but has no deeds? Can such faith save him? Suppose a brother or sister is without clothes and daily food. If one of you says to him, "Go, I wish you well; keep warm and well fed," but does nothing about his physical needs, what good is it? In the same way, faith by itself, if it is not accompanied by action, is dead.

—James 2:14-17

This scripture is a good reminder that we must walk in our faith, take that step of action. Furthermore, we all, in our own circumstances, have different steps to take. Some days, it is easy to look at others and think, *Well, God, why can't I take someone else's step . . . 'cause their step looks a whole lot easier.* That is known as envy, and it is sin.

Remember that we are all uniquely designed and given what God has ordained, including gifts, trials, etc. To envy what someone else has is to *not* acknowledge what God has given *you*. *He gives and He takes away.*

Situations always appear easier when we are not in them and when it is not our walk. I just want to send out a word of encouragement, that "We live by faith, and not by sight" (2 Corinthians 5:7). Don't be afraid to take the step that God is calling you to take no matter what it looks like with your eyes, what you think you know in your head, or how your heart may feel about it.

His ways are not our ways; His thoughts, not our thoughts. Supernatural steps of faith most likely will not play out when analyzed logically or if you try to reason it out within yourself. If it did, it probably would not be a step of faith in Him.

God's people are under attack. I am praying that each of you—in your circumstance, in your valley, on your mountaintop, in your desert, in your oasis—can *boldly* walk in your faith today!

Why Am I Alive?

(To my father, I am so grateful that you did adopt me and I love you! To my biological father, I am grateful for your life. Without you, I would not be here. I am trying to walk the righteous path and I love you too! Both of you are a very important part of my life and testimony!)

My birthday is coming up in a few weeks, and it has always been a strange day for me. I will be turning thirty-six years old or young, depending on your perspective.

Up until very recently, I felt like my birth was a curse. I grew up feeling like my mother never wanted me, and I was some big mistake that really inconvenienced her life after she was married. I think I was ten when she tied the knot. I had been told stories of how I was born out of some hippie commune in Wisconsin but never really got the details. My biological father was much younger than she was, and I was told that he split when I was a year and a half with no real details about that situation either. This always left me feeling like he didn't want me. There are so many things that did not and still do not make sense.

The early days of grunge were a time of musical awakening for me. The scene exploded when I was a vocal performance major in college. Someone had turned my pain and my anger into an expression that touched me at the very core and depths of my being.

By day or, at least, for a few hours of sobriety while the sun was shining, I was singing arias in Italian, French, and sometimes German while trapped in a soundproof booth, which I used to call my piano cell. By night, I was swigging down beer, smoking all sorts of things, and belting out the latest tunes while one of my roommates played his drums with the occasional guitar player for some added accompaniment.

There was something about that music, that audible pain, that always cut me right to the heart—a pain I could relate to. I guess the post-high school years are normally a time when one does question their purpose in life. For me, it was a whole other thing completely on a much deeper level.

In my life thus far, I have never found anyone else who was adopted as a teenager. Even my ex-husband, who told me he was put into the system at the age of nine, still had contact with his biological family. I really didn't.

I have vivid memories, before the age of twelve, of my biological family. I remember my aunts, my mother's sisters, and their husbands and children. I remember how all my cousins at Christmas always got so much more than I did, and how that made me feel inadequate like I was not good enough or deserving of the same goodness that everyone else got. I remember sneaking around, drinking the rest of the wine left in all the adult glasses. I remember when my grandfather, Pap-Pap, died and going to his viewing and touching his hand. I remember the smell of cigarettes on my grandmother's hands and her soft, curly grey hair and how she drank tea with milk and sugar. I remember visiting my biological father and the farm he lived on with chickens and the big red barn and playing with his other children—my two half brothers and half sister.

After my adoption, I remember my one aunt and grandmother coming to visit me once at my dad's house. I remember a few phone calls, but it was like they all disappeared—almost like I disappeared. It was like Julie Gondek ceased to be when I became Julie Petrie. My adoption took the concept of abandonment to a whole new level and created this belief within me that I was unlovable, undeserving, and unworthy of anything good. It somehow reinforced the thought that I was a mistake, and that I deserved everything bad that ever happened to me.

It is no wonder that I ended up in such a mess as an adult before God snatched me up. For years, the enemy had me bound in negativity, self-loathing, and codependency. I always wondered why I was alive, why I was ever born, and why God would have saved me from death by my own hands or those of others.

Imagine my surprise in my membership class at church when the book we were reading announced that I was not a mistake. It was a shock. I remember, at first, after I rededicated my life to Him, it was kind of hard to believe that God really did love me, and that He would never leave me.

Now I know the truth, and the truth really has set me free or is continually setting me free. The more I read scripture, the more truth is revealed and the more I am changed! Slowly God has begun to show me who I am in Him—that I have been adopted again for the second time. He has shown me that I am a new creation, that He loves me, and that I am not a mistake!

I know now why I am still alive, and I know that everything I have been through is for a purpose. I am grateful for my life now, and I give God the glory for the change He has brought about in me.

I used to make respectable ladies clutch their pearls, and my mouth could have made a trucker blush. I thank God for making me new and making me see who I really am and all that I can become in Him.

For those reading this that don't have a relationship with God or don't believe in Him or those that grew up without a father or without a healthy relationship with your father, please know that He wants to adopt you as well. He wants to reveal Himself to you no matter what others have done to you in this life. God will be faithful and never let you down.

> Both the one who makes men holy and those who are made holy are of the same family. So Jesus is not ashamed to call them brothers. (Hebrews 2:11)

> He chose to give us birth through the word of truth, that we might be a kind of firstfruits of all he created. (James 1:18)

> Yet to all who received Him, to those who believed in his name, he gave the right to become children of God—children born not of natural descent, nor of human decision or a husband's will, but born of God. (John 1:12-13)

> Therefore, if anyone is in Christ, he is a new creation; the old has gone, the new has come! (2 Corinthians 5:17)

> He predestined us to be adopted as his sons through Jesus Christ, in accordance with his pleasure and will. (Ephesians 1:5)

Remember, your life has purpose, and you are not a mistake!

DANIEL: MAN OF FAITH

Daniel chapter 6 is all about faith. Daniel was a true godly man of unbelievable faith. In reading it, something struck me.

Verse 3 (NKJV) says, "Then this Daniel distinguished himself above the governors and satraps, because an excellent spirit was in him; and the king gave thought to setting him over the whole realm."

It says he had an excellent spirit in him and distinguished himself to the point where the king was going to set him over the whole kingdom, per the New King James Version. The NIV says he had exceptional qualities. Then we know what happened next. Naturally, others began to notice and sought to destroy him by bringing charges and such.

How often is life like that? When we begin to excel, others, whether they are believers or not, may become jealous or insecure even the very people who we care about most, our coworkers who we thought were friends, the friends from childhood, and the sister or brother that always wants to compete against you. People, including those we love, may not always be happy for our success or our desire to excel, but doesn't that have more to do with them than with us?

Are we not called as children of the Almighty to be distinguished and set apart? Isn't the world supposed to notice something different about us, to see that difference in our actions, not just our words and they way we treat one another?

My dad always said "water seeks its own level." Think of the positive influence we can have if we raise the level, raise the expectation by pulling our brothers and sisters along, lifting them up regardless of how they may feel about us. Could it be that God is using the excellence in you to spur someone else along?

If we do all things as unto the Lord and strive for that excellent Spirit that Daniel had—pray to be filled more and more with the Holy Spirit, walk the righteous path, walk uprightly before the Lord, remain firm and unmovable in our faith in God and not man as Daniel was, and seek to display the exceptional qualities of the Spirit—then there can be no destruction! Make it a point to spur someone else along today!

Some Days, I am Five

But you have not so learned Christ, if indeed you have heard Him
and have been taught by Him, as the truth is in Jesus: that you put off,
concerning your former conduct, the old man which grows corrupt
according to the deceitful lusts, and be renewed in the spirit of your
mind, and that you put on the new man which was created according
to God, in true righteousness and holiness.
                                   —Ephesians 4:20-24, NKJV

I walked into a local Pentecostal Church of God for the first time in January
of 2005. It was not long after my now ex-husband had gone back to jail, and I
had found out that he was involved in a serious relationship with another woman.
My life was a mess, but I knew God was calling me back to Him.

I had grown up in a church similar to this one, so I knew what a Pentecostal,
charismatic service was all about. The church where I was first born again as a
child was also Pentecostal in every way. I can remember as that child, before the
age of around ten, when my biological mother got married and we converted
to Catholicism, accepting Jesus into my heart and knowing what it meant. I
remember being baptized in full water immersion before my toes could reach
the bottom and understanding the significance of that baptism. I remember
speaking in tongues, dancing around the altar in worship, and being slain in
the Spirit in my youth.

As a kid, I remember the big music festivals, and I vividly remember the big
rainbow that outlined the stage. I remember going to retreats at a local camp and
revivals at a local Christian college. I even remember a trip down South to visit
the campground run by a popular TV evangelist of the day. We also visited the set
of his program, but we did not see a taping. I remember being in the studio.

At the church of my youth, I remember being the lead in "Twinkle," the
story of the Bethlehem star during one Christmas season. I remember there

---

were a lot of lines and a lot of songs to learn. I can remember the lights shining so brightly in my eyes and not being able to see anyone in the blackness of the audience.

I remember one service where an evangelist was speaking, and I began to cry for the people who were going to go to hell. The service stopped, and I remember him asking me why I was crying. I remember speaking into the microphone and telling him about my sorrow for the lost souls. I never imagined that I would grow up and become one of those lost souls for whom I had shed tears at such an early age.

At any rate, there was nothing shocking to me about the singing and clapping at this new church or even people speaking in tongues that January day. I felt like the prodigal daughter who had returned home again.

At my first service, two women sang a beautiful song, which reduced me to tears. I knew the way I had been living my life was so wrong and so empty, but that with God, I would be okay. I knew what I had to do.

I remember going down to the altar and rededicating my life to Christ with the senior pastor, barely able to pray and talk through the tears. It was the second time I was born again.

Thus began the renewing process just like in Ephesians. All the years of junk, evil, and sin had taken its toll, but God slowly has been working stuff out.

However, I never could have imagined that being born again as an adult, on that January day, was really going to be just like being born all over again with all the stages and phases that you normally go through growing up.

People throw the terms around all the time: "baby Christian" and "spiritually mature." Well, I must confess that, some days, I am five. I found myself recently acting exactly like a five year old, being kind of like a kindergartner Christian.

It was before I was switched over to the alto section when it was first suggested to me that this section change might happen. What? I quickly did the math in my head and figured out exactly how many years, months, weeks, and days I had been a second soprano. I was going through the choir radio station that plays in my head, tallying all the songs that I had learned, all the splits, scanning in my head the song books, and reviewing the notes where we sing just melody in unison with the firsts, where the first sopranos go up, where the seconds have the melody line, and where we go below—a Bb here, they go to the F, on and on and on.

I was completely consumed by the number of new alto lines that I would have to learn all in a panic, how I was going to relearn the songs and new harmonies, and not to mention learn the new praise team music, music for our women's small group, and another small ensemble that I had been singing with. I was on music overload, or so I thought. I was overwhelmed before anything even happened.

I was having my own temper tantrum in my head, flailing around on the floor of the throne room in front of God. I went running to my Abba to pitch a royal fit just like a kid. I was stomping my spiritual feet. "God, why me? Do I have to? Why not somebody else? Someone newer who doesn't know as many songs?" Thank you, God, for your patience!

It seemed like switching sections in choir was going to be this huge, monumental change, teetering on the edge of a life crisis at the time. Then it actually happened, and I became an alto for the church choir. One night, I made the walk across the second row, serenaded by the choir. They sang "Goodnight, sweetheart. Well, it's time go" as I left my chair, walked past the tenors, and joined the altos in my new seat.

It is okay and not a big deal at all. It has been a month, maybe even two, and the reality of learning the new lines, while challenging, is not overwhelming me, at least not yet. I mess up and make mistakes, but it is like the songs are completely new just like how God is making me completely new.

In life, sometimes change or circumstances can seem overwhelming when, in reality, it may not be anything at all or anything that you think it will be. God may be using change or a circumstance in your life to make you new.

> Therefore, if anyone is in Christ, he is a new creation; the old has gone, the new has come! All this is from God, who reconciled us to Himself through Christ and gave us the ministry of reconciliation: that God was reconciling the world to Himself in Christ, not counting men's sins against them. And he has committed to us the message of reconciliation. We are therefore Christ's ambassadors, as though God were making his appeal through us. We implore you on Christ's behalf: Be reconciled to God. (2 Corinthians 5:17-20, NIV)

I can assure you that it is only through my reconciliation with God that any of the change in me has happened. He wants you to be reconciled today! He can make you new if you let Him!

GET ALONG

One morning, at around four AM, I woke up terribly chipper with an old song lyric from the '80s going through my head in a continuous loop. Considering that I am not a morning person, it was a little more than irritating.

However, I started to ponder the lyrics of the entire song because the more I woke up, the more profound they became. Basically, the song questioned why people can't get along.

So often, we do not even realize what we have done to others or do not remember exactly what others have done to us, and yet we exist in a state of not getting along. The Bible tells us we are to love our enemies, and we are to pray for them even if we do not know why we are not getting along and even if we are not quite sure what happened to make a rift in the first place.

We could be like the world—hold grudges and hang on to our anger, disappointment, and dismay with others like we have some kind of right to be angry—but the Bible calls for something else entirely. We are commanded to love one another, not to be angry with each other. We are not to quarrel or complain. We are commanded to join together in unity not to hold grudges or let bitterness take root. We are to forgive those who have hurt us immeasurably, even the very people who cause us such excruciating pain that you wonder if you will even be able take another breath . . . especially them.

We are all just people, and we all fall short of the glory. We all need His new mercies every morning. We need to extend the grace that God gives us to others. We need to turn the other cheek.

It struck me, as I began to pray for all who have hurt me, that I did not have too much to say, which—for anyone who knows me—is a rarity. Jesus's words then came to mind: "Forgive them, Father, for they know not what they do." So often, I think people just don't know that what they do may be hurting others. Sometimes, they do, but I would guess that, more often than not, people fail to realize the true impact of their actions and words.

Fast forward to nine AM, five long hours later. *Yawn!* My calendar at work had this week's scripture Jeremiah 9:24:

> "but let Him who boasts boast about this: that he understands and knows me, that I am the Lord, who exercises kindness, justice and righteousness on earth, for in these I delight."

That was exactly what I needed to see today. It is not my place to worry about what others have done to me as God is a just God and will deal with them. I just need to ask forgiveness for the things I have done to others and continue to try my very best to live my life righteously, according to the Word and showing kindness to all. Above all, I must stay focused on the Almighty.

Politics

With all the e-mails and discussions flying around about politics these days, I am reminded that Jesus never did really discuss them directly. He did, however, have to deal with the tricks and schemes of the religious politicians of His day who were constantly trying to trap Him in His words.

> Then the Pharisees went out and laid plans to trap Him in His words. They sent their disciples to Him along with the Herodians. "Teacher," they said, "we know you are a man of integrity and that you teach the way of God in accordance with the truth. You aren't swayed by men, because you pay no attention to who they are. Tell us then, what is your opinion? Is it right to pay taxes to Caesar or not?" But Jesus, knowing their evil intent, said, "You hypocrites, why are you trying to trap me? Show me the coin used for paying the tax." They brought Him a denarius, and He asked them, "Whose portrait is this? And whose inscription?" "Caesar's," they replied. Then He said to them, "Give to Caesar what is Caesar's, and to God what is God's." When they heard this, they were amazed. So they left Him and went away. (Matthew 22:15-22)

The Pharisees were opposed to the Roman occupation of Palestine. The Herodians supported Herod Antipas and the policies implemented by Rome. Normally, these two groups hated one another, but they united in a scheme against Jesus.

How many of you can testify that God the Father, the Son, and the Holy Spirit, my Holy Trinity, is stronger than any scheme man could possibly dream up? Their intentions and motivations were anything but pure or holy in asking Jesus this question about taxes, and He knew it, knew exactly what they were trying to do, and exposed them. The scripture in 1 Corinthians 4:5 says, ". . .

He will bring to light things hidden in darkness and will expose the motives of men's hearts . . ."

No matter what tricks and schemes of man you may be dealing with, just know that God is in control.

It Is You, Lord

You Are All I Need

REJECTION AND CONVICTION

Section I

> Do not waste yourself in rejection; do no bark against the bad, but chant the beauty of the good.
> —Ralph Waldo Emerson

> I never saw a wild thing sorry for itself. A small bird will drop frozen from a bough without ever having felt sorry for itself.
> —D. H. Lawrence

> The stone the builders rejected has become the capstone.
> —Psalms 118:22

> See I lay a stone in Zion, a tested stone, a precious cornerstone for a sure foundation; the one who trusts will never be dismayed.
> —Isaiah 28:16

> He will be a stone that causes men to stumble
> —Isaiah 8:14

No one living either in the past, present, or future could possibly have suffered the rejection Jesus, Son of God and Son of Man, felt during his time here on this fragile globe. Nor did He feel sorry for Himself. His rejection was not wasted but provided us a way to the Father.

Jesus knew who He was, and yet I wonder if the rejection He suffered was any less painful. Somehow I doubt it. Is there a way to deal with the pain of rejection without feeling sorry for yourself? I believe there is, and that we can follow the example of Jesus.

Step 1. Surround yourself with those who love you and care about you and are willing to keep watch and pray with you. Jesus took his closest companions to the Garden of Gethsemane: Peter, James, and John. They were also on the mountaintop with Him during the Transfiguration.

Step 2. Self-awareness. Do you know your God-given purpose in life? Do you know what the consequences of living out your destiny will be? Jesus Himself would quote Psalms 118 (see Matthew 21:42, Mark 12:10, and Luke 20:17) as part of the Parable of the Tenants. Moreover, He knew that He was the fulfillment of that scripture.

Step 3. You have no need to defend yourself or justify yourself to those who would reject you. Jesus never did.

The teachers of the law and the chief priests immediately began to look for a way to arrest Jesus because they knew He had spoken the Parable of the Tenants against them.

There will be those who will rise up against you. Their rejection may be a reaction to their own conviction brought about by a move of the Holy Spirit.

Conviction seems to produce an overwhelming sense of anger, shame, and guilt all at the same time. Yet within the stone-hearted person, there remains an unwillingness to examine themselves and an unyielded spirit. Even within the heart of flesh of fellow believers, conviction has the power of the Spirit to change us, but only if we allow it. Their rejection of you may have very little to do with you and much more do with them.

Section II

There are moments in life when we all must make a choice: to deny Christ in action, thought, or deed or choose to follow Him. Sometimes these choices are easy. You may choose to bow your head in a public place to say grace before a meal. However, sometimes the choices are very hard as your own family or close friends may not approve of your righteous and holy living. They may verbally tease you, discretely reject you, or angrily curse your beliefs, which is just conviction.

Take heart if you've ever experienced rejection in any form due to your faith.

Luke 14:26 speaks volumes.

"If anyone comes to me and does not hate his father and mother, his wife and children, his brothers and sisters—yes, even his own life—he cannot be my disciple. And anyone who does not carry his cross and follow me cannot be my disciple."

Like Peter, we must also count the cost of what being a follower of Christ really means. Just like Peter, it is easy to have zealous statements and proclaim to the world that you are saved. It is easy to say you are not ashamed, but do you have the courage, when the time comes, to speak the truth of the Word? When faced with real world and everyday life decisions, sometimes it is not so easy, and the cost becomes very real.

What if your entire family refused to have anything to do with you because you are a Christian? In other countries, they have the threat of guns to their heads and endure persecution for being a Christian. The threat of losing one's life is very real in parts of the world, but what if the gun, for you, is the threat of isolation from those you love? Never to see your mother again, never to speak to your father again, never to see your siblings grow up? What then? What choice would you make?

God is a jealous God, and to really follow Him, nothing and no one can be more important. Family, friends, careers, houses, cars, and bank accounts cannot take precedence.

Mother's Day

(To my biological mother. Though she may never read this, I still want her to know that I love her and thank God for her!)

In Psalms 27: 9-10, David cried out:

> Do not hide your face from me, do not turn your servant away in anger; you have been my helper. Do not reject me or forsake me, O God my Savior. Though my father and mother forsake me, the *Lord* will receive me.

This scripture is particularly meaningful as I was given up for adoption around the age of twelve. I had run away from home to the house of my best friend at the time as things between my mother, her husband, and me were not right.

My best friend's father eventually took me in and then adopted me about a year later. Through high school, my mother and I did not have much contact until my maternal grandmother died during my first year of college. I then reached out and attempted to have a relationship with her, and over the next fifteen years, we would speak occasionally. Sometimes we would spend small amounts of time together, but I always felt I was the one seeking her out and working the relationship.

The last time I saw her was over lunch with her and my two aunts. She was distant and reticent. That was in February of 2002.

Her most recent and final rejection of me came this past Mothers' Day when I located her via a web search. I sent her a Christian e-card saying that I never wanted her to stop being my mom, that I loved her and forgave her. There was no response. When I went to e-mail her one of the gem devotionals several days later, she had changed her e-mail address.

God does promise that He will not forsake us or leave us, and there, in Psalms 27, I believe God is whispering that He will receive us regardless of who else abandons us whether it be a mother, a husband, a brother, a sister, or a friend. No matter what or who on earth we seek not to lose, only He has the power to give and take away.

Sometimes, when God prunes our lives, what He takes away is for our good. It very well may also be that, when we feel rejected, it has nothing to do with who we are, and God may be simply working something out in them.

Bohemian Ideals

Bohemian quips are everywhere. One, found on my coffee cup, struck me in particular. The point of the quote was that it is most important in this life to have real love, truth, and stability.

While this bohemian answer of what is most important in life may be the popular world view and how most people would answer, it fails to recognize the only constant, the only important thing in life, which is God. Love, truth, and stability are all nice concepts, but without God, I would say that they really don't exist because God is love, God is truth, and God is the only unchanging, stable thing in this crazy world.

Over the course of last week, I moved into a new apartment (a box-filled mess at the moment), sold a car (good-bye black car with the banging system), went on a two-day business trip to Pittsburgh that took more than ten hours of driving for a one-hour business lunch (though I am thankful for the experience), and left the next day on a four-day outreach to Texas with my choir, doing some musical missionary work.

If I relied on the world's standards of stability, my life, particularly with all its recent events, would not appear to be stable. But God . . . With God—as my solid Rock, as my source of truth, and my source of soul-sustaining love—I can rest in Him. For He makes me lie down in the green pastures and provides all the comfort I need.

That is my prayer for all of you today, that you all be refreshed and renewed by the life-giving power of God and His Spirit. Jesus is the only way, the only truth, and the only way to life, abundant and everlasting. I also pray that you find all the stability you are looking for in the Rock!

Be Still or Move?

The Lord will fight for you; you need only to be still.

—Exodus 14:14

Be still before the Lord and wait patiently for Him; do not fret when men succeed in their ways, when they carry out their wicked schemes.

—Psalms 37:7

Be still, and know that I am God; I will be exalted among the nations, I will be exalted in the earth.

—Psalms 46:10

I have a hard time being still.

Physically, I am just generally moving around. When I hear music whether externally or internally, I am immediately in motion. I also fidget a lot and sometimes end up playing with my pen or tapping my toes. There is not a whole lot of stillness.

Mentally, my thoughts race around the never-ending track in my head with the things of life like schedules, priorities, bills, work, and all the other general stuff. Then the other track is busy contemplating the things of God: His goodness, kingdom work, the monthly schedule for ministering in song, spiritual priorities, the Word, the plans He has for me, people I need to pray for, to be in the presence, and to freely worship in spirit and truth.

Somehow, I have managed to learn how to force myself to be still before God outside the times of public and private worship, but it is a hard thing for me. The quieting of the external environment is the easy thing for me at this point in my walk. There is no cable TV to turn off, and it is more than easy to turn off the rehearsal CD. Then comes the biggest challenge: to be quiet internally, to have the internal thoughts turned off, to turn off the internal music that dances through my mind almost constantly and not hear the rhythm of life, and finally to be able to truly focus on Him.

Psalms 46 was written by the sons of Korah, and if you read the whole chapter, it is going along, talking about how God is our refuge and strength so we do not have to fear (Amen!). It continues with singing the praise of our Lord, the whole way down until that verse 10. Then, out of the blue, there are quotation marks like God Himself was all of a sudden there with the author, speaking directly to Him. This stillness to me is all about the reverence for the Almighty who is sovereign over all things. "Be still, and know that I am God; I will be exalted among the nations, I will be exalted in the earth." (Psalms 46:10)

Psalms 37 was written by David and talks about being still in another context entirely. My lunch crew was just discussing this very thing the other day. "Why do bad people seem to get away with stuff?" People say "what comes around goes around," but sometimes we don't see the negative results of the evil ones who seem to prosper. However, God knows everything and sees all! This being quiet, I believe, has something to do with allowing God to handle those who have hurt us, again recognizing His sovereignty in all situations. Be still before the Lord and wait patiently for Him; do not fret when men succeed in their ways when they carry out their wicked schemes. (Psalms 37:7)

The Exodus scripture actually in context is quite interesting. When the Israelites saw the Egyptians and pharaoh approaching, Moses says to his people, "The Lord will fight for you; you need only to be still." Moses was saying, "Don't be afraid, God will deliver us and fight for us." But God answers Moses and tells him to have the Israelites move on, and that he is to stretch his hand over the sea. So while Moses was telling them to be still, God wanted them to move and take action.

As in all things, it is always a wise decision to allow God to direct your path and allow Him to speak to your heart whether *He* wants you to stop dead in your tracks and be still or if He wants you to move. I also encourage you to take some quiet time everyday before the Lord in reverence and stillness to exalt His sovereignty in your life. When the wicked prosper and succeed in their evil ways, just *be* still and watch God work it out.

HOPE

My focus lately has been on hope as we all need hope. I have been reminded that only God can truly be the provider of that hope. True hope cannot come from your mom, dad, spouse, or friend, and not from anyone or anything in this world.

This is my prayer for all of you:

> May the God of hope fill you with all joy and peace as you trust in Him, so that you may overflow with hope by the power of the Holy Spirit. (Romans 15:13)

> Because God wanted to make the unchanging nature of his purpose very clear to the heirs of what was promised, he confirmed it with an oath. God did this so that, by two unchangeable things in which it is impossible for God to lie, we who have fled to take hold of the hope offered to us may be greatly encouraged. We have this hope as an anchor for the soul, firm and secure. It enters the inner sanctuary behind the curtain. (Hebrews 6:17-19)

I just kept reading this Hebrews scripture over and over again as it contains so many amazing parts. Let me start in the middle verse that says God cannot lie: *"It is impossible for God to lie."* He reveals to us a part of His very nature in this scripture, part of who He is. He is trustworthy. Man will disappoint and let you down every time, but God will not.

Do you believe this? Do you really? Do you know that He will catch you when you fall? Spiritual check! I had to ask myself these questions several times and really meditate upon this. Do your actions show that you believe that God cannot lie in your daily walk?

Satan himself is the only author of confusion and lies, and he is sneaky. Therefore, sometimes it easy to believe the lies he would tangle your mind with, and it becomes easy to believe lies about others. However, I pray that each of you, as you read this, will let God reveal His trustworthiness in your lives and grant you the knowledge to know the truth and believe the truth because He is the way, He is the truth.

"He wanted to make the unchanging nature of His purpose very clear." His nature does not change; He is the same today, yesterday, and always! Regardless of our behavior, our sin, our human weaknesses, or our bad decisions, He loves us no matter what, and I pray that you feel His love today because He has a purpose for you.

"To the heirs." We are those heirs. Do you know who you are? Do you know who God says you are? Remind yourself today that you are God's princess or God's prince, and that you are a son or daughter of the Almighty. Do you walk in your position? Do you know your purpose?

"Take hold of the hope offered to us, [so we] may be greatly encouraged." This grabbed my attention simply because it implies that we must be an active part of our own encouragement. We need to take hold and grab on to that hope offered to us. It is not a passive act.

"We have this hope as an anchor for the soul, firm and secure." This is so beautiful. This hope is an anchor for our souls. It is firm and immovable. It is safe and secure. We can cry out, "Abba, Father."

For me, having never known safety or security while growing up and even as an adult for that matter until January 2005, it becomes a struggle sometimes to rest in my Heavenly Father and know that He will provide that security. I pray that you will feel His hope today and let it be an anchor for your soul.

More Than You Can Bear

I will share with everyone that Tuesday was the best day I've had in a long time. We started recording again the original music for *Gems from the Jewelry Box: The Reason* with the melodies and lyrics that God has blessed me with. It had been approximately seven and a half months since our last attempt at recording. It was the mountaintop that was equal to Mount Everest. I was on top of the world. I was tired and exhausted but filled with such joy, satisfaction, happiness, and peace.

I woke up this Wednesday morning, and the sun was shining. The birds were singing me a symphony. The sky was blue and beautiful, and I still was left with a grin from ear to ear.

I went to work basking in the afterglow. No one knew of the mountaintop I had been on, but they could tell, by looking at me, that something great had happened. When I tried to share, no one cared, and no one really wanted to hear my news or listen to the fruits of our labor—the scratch track that KC and I had worked so hard on.

The workday got crazy very quickly with phones ringing off the hook, cases flying around, raised voices here and there. It is a rare day for it to be really awful at the office, but today was one of those days. My mountaintop became the lowest valley all in the span of just a few hours. So what happened to the joy that no one could take away?

I think it got buried by the never-ending phone calls today, the presentation I had to do for my boss when my mind was not anywhere near the office or even what I was talking about, the e-mails that piled up all the way over my head, and the messages from yesterday still waiting to be answered. It was all this junk and office stuff that really took its toll on me today.

I went in search of a scripture after a very long day. I came upon John 16. Jesus tells the disciples that He is leaving them and going to the Father. Jesus tells them, in verse 12, "I have much more to say to you, more than you can now bear."

This part of the scripture hit me in a different way tonight as I read it. Jesus had so much to tell them, but it would have been too much for them to deal with at the time. People always say, in difficult times, He never gives us more than we can bear. While this thought is comforting in some sense, the stuff of life can be so overwhelming at times; the truth of the matter is that the concept is hard to accept.

When Jesus spoke these words, He knew it was only a few hours before his death, but at the same time, only days away from His resurrection. So I ponder His words differently tonight. As I sit here and process the day's events, I remember how I felt my joy slowly slipping away minute by minute. It makes me wonder what else Jesus cannot show me or reveal to me because I was unable to place things in their proper perspective today. It makes me realize how the enemy just crept in today and yanked the rug right out from under me, and I even felt it happening. I went and prayed in the midst of my descent but, still, down the mountain I tumbled.

I have also noticed that, when I get overly tired, my old mouth seems to want to rear its ugly head. I get frustrated so easily, and the comments fly. I know this about myself, and still it happens despite my numerous conversations with God about my mouth. I failed that test again tonight! Thank God His mercies are new every morning!

Maybe the issue is that the feelings on the mountaintop and the feelings in the valley are really just distortions of our own perceptions of the situation; that God defines the truth of the situation regardless of how we feel or do not feel. If I really believe that this scripture is true, then why did I let myself get all stressed out about stuff that God thinks that I can handle?

Be blessed in whatever you are presently facing and know that God really won't give you more than you can bear. Jump three days ahead in your own situation. Is your miracle waiting for you just days away? God knows what lies ahead. Your current circumstance, challenge, or weakness could be building character for some future point in time.

RULES OF A CHRISTIAN HOUSEHOLD

Paul writes the rules for Christian households in Colossian 3:18-21 (NIV) and they are as follows:

1. Wives, submit to your husbands, as is fitting in the Lord.
2. Husbands, love your wives and do not be harsh with them.
3. Children, obey your parents in everything as this pleases the Lord.
4. Fathers (and Mothers), do not embitter your children, or they will become discouraged.

In my life thus far, I have been a mother, a wife, and obviously a child, but none of it really being in a Christian household or Christian environment. I learned a lot from these experiences: mostly what a marriage is not, what a wife is not, surely what a husband is not, what parents are not, and what a child should not do.

As a mother to my second fiancé's children for about two years, I learned that, no matter how much I loved his children, I could not save them. His son had numerous medical problems, and although I was a nurse, it was hard to be on the other side of the bed. I was helpless. His daughter had numerous behavioral issues from all the instability in her short life. I saw myself in her and wanted so desperately to let her know that she was loved. I wanted to be the mother to her that I never had.

As a wife, even after I rededicated my heart to the Lord, I learned that I could not save my husband or change him nor was I responsible for his evil behavior. His infidelity was not a reflection on me. This was hard to believe when, all my life, I was programmed to believe everything I went through was my fault. I learned that I could not look to my now ex-husband to fulfill me, and that it did not matter how much I gave as there was no end to his taking.

111

As a child, I was very rebellious, acting out and angry at all the things that had happened to me before the age of twelve, and I turned it all inward. I remember trying to kill myself in seventh or eighth grade. I took a whole bunch of pills and drank a whole bunch of alcohol. I called my boyfriend at the time, and he rode his bike over to my house with one of his friends. They kept me awake or tried to, and I can remember them trying to make me walk and drink water. I remember them leaving so my mom would not catch them at the house. When she got home, my mother was completely oblivious that anything was wrong with me. I must have left enough pills and enough liquor so they were not missed and must not have taken enough to go into a coma.

After all that codependency and mess, it is amazing how God kept His hand on me and has changed me, renewed me, and transformed me as He will continue to do until He takes me home. The deeper my walk, the harder the changes seem to get.

It strikes me that my relationship with God is the first right relationship in my life. It is the first trusting relationship, the first relationship where I have loved and been loved back unconditionally, the first relationship where my needs have been fulfilled, and where all He wants from me is my attention, my devotion, my faith, and my love.

I pray for marriages and families on a daily basis. I never saw a healthy, functional family growing up, so I never had that model to learn from. Now, as a Christian adult, I learn from God, the Spirit, and from all of you. I see the way that husbands treat their wives, and wives, I see how you treat your husbands. Parents, I see the way you treat your children. I thank God for the Christian family I am now blessed with filled with a spiritual mother and many friends who mean more to me than they will ever know.

Those four simple sentences, above, from Paul seem so basic. I will continue my prayers as I believe marriages and families are truly under attack. We are no different than the Romans, and the enemy is attempting to destroy us from the inside out.

The Rock

He Called to Me

WHO IS GOING TO THE MOUNTAINTOP WITH YOU?

After six days Jesus took Peter, James and John with Him and led them up a high mountain, where they were all alone. There he was transfigured before them. His clothes became dazzling white, whiter than anyone in the world could bleach them. And there appeared before them Elijah and Moses, who were talking with Jesus.

Peter said to Jesus, "Rabbi, it is good for us to be here. Let us put up three shelters—one for you, one for Moses and one for Elijah." [He did not know what to say, they were so frightened.]

Then a cloud appeared and enveloped them, and a voice came from the cloud: "This is my Son, whom I love. Listen to Him!"
—Mark 9:2-7, The Transfiguration

In Matthew's account of The Transfiguration which is found in chapter 17, the apostles fall to the ground in fear after the presence of the Almighty appeared and spoke. Jesus goes to them, touches them, and tells them in verse seven, "Do not be afraid."

Suddenly, when they looked around, they no longer saw anyone with them except Jesus.

As they were coming down the mountain, Jesus gave them orders: 'Do not tell anyone what you have seen until the Son of Man has risen from the dead.' (Matthew 17:9) Mark's account says in verse nine, "They kept the matter to themselves, discussing what "rising from the dead" meant."

In my harmony of the Gospels list, the Transfiguration is event no. 111. This is after many miracles have already been performed by Jesus: the turning of water into wine, feeding the five thousand, healing the lame man by the pool, healing Peter's mother-in-law, casting demons out, calming the storm, and walking on water. This was not the first time anything out of the ordinary happened. Yet the three apostles, these three disciples—Peter, James, and John—were still afraid.

It is my assumption that those three were the closest to Jesus for Him to bring them along on this very significant event in His life. That left nine other disciples out of the mix, but all had their purpose and part to play.

Of course, Jesus, being Jesus, knew all three. He knew their faults, strengths, and weaknesses. He knew that Peter would deny Him but also knew that the early church would be built upon that rock—Petras. He knew James and John better than they knew themselves—Zebedee's sons—known as the Sons of Thunder (a little anger management issue perhaps) whose mother would ask Jesus to let her sons sit at His right and left. Jesus would ask John to care for Mary after His death. Jesus knew them, but do you think the three apostles really knew *Him*? Do you think they knew the significance of what they had seen and had been told?

I would encourage all of you to evaluate your own walk and how well you know your Redeemer. How well do you know Him?

In your own lives, are you able to know the faults and weaknesses of those around you, those you are closest to, and still love and accept them as Jesus did? Are you learning from those around you?

Who are you taking to the mountaintop? And do they know the significance they have in your life? Is Jesus walking to the mountaintop with you?

WHAT IS A GOOD WIFE?
WHAT MAKES A GOOD HUSBAND?

Ish is the Hebrew word for husband. It is discussed in Hosea 2:16, 2:19-20:

> "In that day," declares the *Lord*, "you will call me 'my husband' [*Ish*]; you will no longer call me 'my master' . . . I will betroth you to me forever; I will betroth you in righteousness and justice, in love and compassion. I will betroth you in faithfulness, and you will acknowledge the Lord."

How do you treat God? Has *He* really become your husband? Do you desire to please *Him*, do you question *Him*, and is *He* the head of your life?

In my e-mail, I received a copy of a real article from 1955. It had the stereotypical 1950s definition of what a good wife should be: have dinner ready, the kids perfect, the house perfect, don't talk, don't question him, and look good all at the same time. It is more or less an impossible, very dysfunctional definition of what any wife should be.

The 1950s was a very different culture where wives "may" have truly aspired to be like this. However, I wonder if they truly did.

Back then, the family stayed together and prayed together. Divorce was not widely accepted, and by no means was it the cultural norm. There was no birth control pill, and no real daycare in the '50s on a widespread scale. Most families were nuclear, and men were expected to be men, to stand up and be the head of the household. Most women were expected to stay at home, raise the children, take care of the house, and had very limited career choices. Back then, most families went to church together and spent time talking to one another.

We have all seen the reruns of the black-and-white sitcoms of that era. Who doesn't want that perfect, cookie-cutter existence with Mr. and Mrs. Right portraying the perfect model of what a husband, wife, and family should be? The trouble is it is not real! Just like the wife in the 1955 article is not real either.

While these nostalgic, fairy-tale descriptions of what a good wife or a good husband is are somewhat amusing, it should make us pause and really consider what our culture has done to men and women and our roles within our society. I think somehow we have stripped men of their manhood and stripped women of their womanhood throughout the last decades of the twentieth century and continue to do so even into the twenty-first.

Is the TV sitcom to blame? Has the feminist movement done a disservice to the institution of marriage?

The biblical principle exists for equality, but somehow our society has taken the concept far beyond equal pay for the same work. Things are simply out of order.

I do believe marriage is the ultimate partnership, and the enemy has done plenty to destroy it as an institution. Only through Christ will the divorce rate drop, and men return to their rightful place as God intended it to be. Only through Christ will husbands and wives be able to treat one another with mutual respect with a deep-abiding love and faithfulness that cannot be destroyed.

Christ loved the church so much that He died for us. How much do you love your spouse? How many marriages could be happier if people were kinder to one another and showed that kind of unselfishness, to lay one's life down? What would happen if people put Christ at the head of their marriage and the man as the head of the house not to lord over his wife but to be a leader? What would happen if the men in this country stood up and assumed their place as the spiritual head of the household? How many men even want to take their godly place?

I pray, for all of you who are married, that your love for your spouse will be strengthened and renewed, that your marriages will all be blessed. I pray for all who are married and single to let the Lord be your Ish. For our nation, I pray that moral order is restored, and both the family and the institution of marriage are once again valued.

Men, I pray for you—both single and married, saved and unsaved—because this world would try to give you a false sense of what a man should really be and how you should treat a woman. I pray that God reveals the truth to you of who you are in Him.

Women, I pray for us all—my sisters who are single and married, saved and unsaved—that we are able to give men the honor and respect they deserve. We also need to be able to submit to our husbands whether it is the earthly man that God has blessed you with or our Lord, our first husband. I pray that we are all able to truly submit with mutual respect, protection, and love for one another—not in a 1950s unrealistic way but rather in the godly way that He intended.

—

Honor, Hate, and Love

Honor

Jesus said, in Luke 18:29-30 (NIV), "'I tell you the truth,' Jesus said to them, 'no one who has left home or wife or brothers or parents or children for the sake of the kingdom of God will fail to receive many times as much in this age and, in the age to come, eternal life.'" This section in Luke is almost the same as in Matthew 19:16-30.

> Now a man came up to Jesus and asked, "Teacher, what good thing must I do to get eternal life?" "Why do you ask me about what is good?" Jesus replied. "There is only One who is good. If you want to enter life, obey the commandments." "Which ones?" the man inquired. Jesus replied, "Do not murder, do not commit adultery, do not steal, do not give false testimony, honor your father and mother, and love your neighbor as yourself." "All these I have kept," the young man said. "What do I still lack?" Jesus answered, "If you want to be perfect, go, sell your possessions and give to the poor, and you will have treasure in heaven. Then come, follow me." When the young man heard this, he went away sad, because he had great wealth. Then Jesus said to his disciples, "I tell you the truth, it is hard for a rich man to enter the kingdom of heaven. Again I tell you, it is easier for a camel to go through the eye of a needle than for a rich man to enter the kingdom of God. When the disciples heard this, they were greatly astonished and asked, "Who then can be saved?" Jesus looked at them and said, "With man this is impossible, but with God all things are possible." Peter answered Him, "We have left everything to follow you! What then will there be for us?" Jesus said to them, "I tell you the truth, at the renewal

of all things, when the Son of Man sits on his glorious throne, you who have followed me will also sit on twelve thrones, judging the twelve tribes of Israel. And everyone who has left houses or brothers or sisters or father or mother or children or fields for my sake will receive a hundred times as much and will inherit eternal life. But many who are first will be last, and many who are last will be first." (Matthew 19:16-30)

Honor, respect, and reverence—particularly for one's parents—were so important in the Jewish tradition and to the Jews whom Matthew was writing to. There it is in verse 19. Jesus reiterates one of the commandments—"to honor your father and mother." Yet in verse 29, we receive the Word that we may be called to sacrifice many things for the sake of believing in Jesus including possibly the familial relationships with our blood relatives or other possessions, which may be dear to us.

Hate

What about the word *hate* in Luke 14:26: "If anyone comes to me and does not *hate* his father and mother, his wife and children, his brothers and sisters-yes, even his own life-he cannot be my disciple." It is an interesting use of the word particularly since we are commanded to love one another and honor our mothers and fathers. I actually looked the verse up in several different translations, and they all have translated the meaning of the original word as *hate*.

So what does hate really mean here? Is he telling us to hate our mothers and fathers or simply telling us that we must love Him the most and be willing to place *Him* truly above all others?

So how do you not hate but love, honor, and respect those that would spit upon you for your choice to follow Him and lay it all down for Him whether it be family, friends, enemies, or all three?

Romans 12:9 says, "Love must be sincere. Hate what is evil; cling to what is good." Maybe that is the answer. We are to hate the evil behavior in people; but love, honor, and respect them as we are all made in God's image and regardless if they are saved or unsaved for they know not what they do.

Revelations 2:6 says, ". . . You hate the practices of the Nicolaitans, which I also hate." Maybe this scripture gives us another answer. We can hate the practices as well as all other things that God despises like gossip, sexual impurity, and greed but not hate the person.

Romans 13:13 says, "Let us behave decently, as in the daytime, not in orgies and drunkenness, not in sexual immorality and debauchery, not in dissension and jealousy." Colossians 3:5 also says, "Put to death, therefore, whatever belongs to

—

your earthly nature: sexual immorality, impurity, lust, evil desires and greed, which is idolatry." However, we must not hate the people that do these things.

After all, the love we have for one another is how they will know us. We are commanded to love one another in 1 John 3:18 which says "Dear children, let us not love with words or tongue, but with actions and in truth."

Love

> A new command I give you: Love one another. As I have loved you, so you must love one another. By this all men will know that you are my disciples, if you love one another. (John 13:34-35)

> But I tell you who hear me: Love your enemies, do good to those who hate you. (Luke 6:27)

> Hear the word of the Lord, you who tremble at his word: "Your brothers who hate you, and exclude you because of my name, have said, 'Let the Lord be glorified, that we may see your joy!' Yet they will be put to shame." (Isaiah 66:5)

Truly to love Christ more than anything is the place where we need to be, to be swallowed up in our love and devotion to our Savior, to be all consumed by the all-consuming fire:

> I am sending you out like sheep among wolves. Therefore be as shrewd as snakes and as innocent as doves. Be on your guard against men; they will hand you over to the local councils and flog you in their synagogues. On my account you will be brought before governors and kings as witnesses to them and to the Gentiles. But when they arrest you, do not worry about what to say or how to say it. At that time you will be given what to say, for it will not be you speaking, but the Spirit of your Father speaking through you. Brother will betray brother to death, and a father his child; children will rebel against their parents and have them put to death. *All men will hate you because of me, but he who stands firm to the end will be saved.* When you are persecuted in one place, flee to another. I tell you the truth, you will not finish going through the cities of Israel before the Son of Man comes. A student is not above his teacher, nor a servant above his master. It is enough for the student to be like his teacher, and the servant like his master. If the head of the house has been called Beelzebub, how much more the members of his household! So do not be afraid of them. There is

---

nothing concealed that will not be disclosed, or hidden that will not be made known. What I tell you in the dark, speak in the daylight; what is whispered in your ear, proclaim from the roofs.

Do not be afraid of those who kill the body but cannot kill the soul. Rather, be afraid of the one who can destroy both soul and body in hell. Are not two sparrows sold for a penny? Yet not one of them will fall to the ground apart from the will of your Father. And even the very hairs of your head are all numbered. So don't be afraid; you are worth more than many sparrows.

Whoever acknowledges me before men, I will also acknowledge him before my Father in heaven. But whoever disowns me before men, I will disown him before my Father in heaven.

Do not suppose that I have come to bring peace to the earth. I did not come to bring peace, but a sword. For I have come to turn a man against his father, a daughter against her mother, a daughter-in-law against her mother-in-law—a man's enemies will be the members of his own household.

Anyone who loves his father or mother more than me is not worthy of me; anyone who loves his son or daughter more than me is not worthy of me; and anyone who does not take his cross and follow me is not worthy of me. Whoever finds his life will lose it, and whoever loses his life for my sake will find it.

He who receives you receives me, and he who receives me receives the one who sent me. Anyone who receives a prophet because he is a prophet will receive a prophet's reward, and anyone who receives a righteous man because he is a righteous man will receive a righteous man's reward. And if anyone gives even a cup of cold water to one of these little ones because he is my disciple, I tell you the truth, he will certainly not lose his reward. (Matthew 10:16-42; emphasis added)

He Called

The Lord is not slow in keeping his promise, as some understand slowness. He is patient with you, not wanting anyone to perish, but everyone to come to repentance.

—2 Peter 3:9

I took you from the ends of the earth,
    from its farthest corners I called you.
I said, "You are my servant";
    I have chosen you and have not rejected you.

So do not fear, for I am with you;
    do not be dismayed, for I am your God.
I will strengthen you and help you;
    I will uphold you with my righteous right hand.

—Isaiah 41:9-10

I can never keep up with my mail these days whether it be the regular snail mail or e-mail. I have fallen sadly behind on my e-mail devotional readings. This usually happens when the calendar gets busy. The calendar is plenty busy right now with the Christmas choir season.

I was just sitting here tonight, a Monday night, December 17, 2007, and opened up my first piece of snail mail in the pile. It was a devotional and calendar from a nationally known ministry. In the 2008 calendar are scriptures listed for each day. So I decided to turn to today's date for next year and began to pray about the year that lies ahead.

The first scripture above, 2 Peter 3:9, is there for December 17, 2008. It was also the topic of another devotional I read a few days ago that would not leave me alone.

—

Usually, when scriptures won't leave me alone, I cut and paste them into a Word doc. This is how most of these devotionals start, and as usual, where they start is never where they end.

God has been dealing with me lately about my lack of patience. All my life, I have charged ahead and been impulsive and before Christ, there was no patience at all in anything. I wanted to hurry through the good times and good moments to get to the crash at the other end. I was so used to being abandoned, I wanted to race and charge quickly ahead to find the pain that I knew I could expect on the other side.

This leads me to the second verse that a dear sister in Christ sent to me. The very Word of God brought forth through Isaiah had comforted her in her personal trial.

Things, like the calendar moment, happen and remind me that His promises are real, that He hears me and is watching over me and His timing is always perfect, that He will bring about those promises that will save His people, and that He has been ever so patient with me.

The verses in Isaiah echo through the hollow halls of my humble heart: He chose me just as He chose you. We are *His* servants.

My lack of patience, before God, was all about fear and rejection. So now, as He gives me life things to build my patience, that old wineskin way of thinking tries to creep back in: the fear comes, the impatience rises up with any good thing of the moment, waiting for it to be over, the anxious nervousness of waiting to be dropped on my head again stirs within the very depth of my soul, and the doubt of His very promises spoken to me rears its ugly head.

Sometimes, in the midst of all my impatience, I lose sight of the fact that He chose me. Maybe it is because sometimes I forget that despite all those years I was living in the world steeped in sin, He was still there. He was still watching me, and even though I did not recognize Him, see Him, or hear Him because the blinders were still on, He was *there!* He is just like the star that hides behind the cloud but is still there, shining ever so brightly.

It is easy to forget that, just because I made the decision to bow my knee and confess Jesus as my *Lord* one January day in 2005, that action doesn't mean I—all of a sudden—get to choose my purpose or choose my own plan or dictate my agenda and my timeline to the Almighty because now I suddenly see. It is also a good reminder that He chose me simply because He wanted to—not because I deserved it but because He loved me. That is the miracle of His grace.

—

Minister to Him

(To pastors, God bless you all in your ministries as you use your gifts and resources for the kingdom, as you serve others, and as you serve God! Thank you for all that you do! You may never know the effects or outcome of the seeds that you planted, but you are vital to God's work. Special thanks to all who have been pastors to me personally! To the Nations of Praise Choir, Spring Valley Praise Team, Just Worship and One Family, it has been an honor and privilege to minister unto Him alongside all of you. I love you all!)

> And thou shalt give to the priests the Levites that be of the seed of Zadok, which approach unto me, *to minister unto me*, saith the Lord GOD, a young bullock for a sin offering.
> —Ezekiel 43:19, KJV; emphasis added

> You are to give a young bull as a sin offering to the priests, who are Levites, of the family of Zadok, who come near *to minister before me*, declares the Sovereign Lord.
> —Ezekiel 43:19, NIV; emphasis added

> You shall give a young bull for a sin offering to the priests, the Levites, who are of the seed of Zadok, who approach me *to minister to me*, says the Lord God.
> —Ezekiel 43:19, NKJV; emphasis added

When I originally read it, it was in the New King James Version, and the words *minister unto me* came jumping off the page at me. I wanted to see what the other translations had to say.

This chapter in Ezekiel is about the glory of the Lord returning to the temple. This part of the chapter specifically deals with the altar and offerings that were to be made.

The idea of ministering *to* God just strikes me. I know we are created to praise Him, to worship Him, and I have often thought of music in terms of ministering a song or ministering in praise—singing for God—but I never really thought of myself as ministering *to* God. I have often been in His presence, worshiped at the foot of the throne, poured my praise upon Him, but minister *to* Him, *directly to Him?* Who me?

Even if you don't sing, have you ever considered that you are ministering to God? You minister to God simply by using whatever talents or gifts He has given you. No gift is too small, and what you give back to God is pleasing to Him. What has God burned into the very depths of your soul to do for Him? How does God want you to minister to Him and His people?

Along with the idea of ministering to Him goes the approaching of God or coming near to Him. You must be near to minister. You can approach God through praise, worship, prayer, reading His Word, and giving of yourself to others. There are countless ways, and God is a personal God. I encourage all of you to approach and get as near as you can to the Almighty and minister to Him today in a way that is personally meaningful to you and to Him. Oh to be in that shadow!

No Fear

I confess that I am afraid to sing solos. My heart starts going eighty-five thousand miles a minute, my hands shake, the sweat comes pouring out of me, and I generally feel like I am going to throw up. It is quite a whole thing and not really a pleasant experience.

The thing of it is that I was never afraid to sing solos before rededicating my life to Christ. Why all this fear? It is a question I have pondered and taken before the Lord numerous times.

Through this one issue, I have come to the realization that I have lived most of my life in fear, about many different things. I suppose it comes from the abandonment and instability growing up and then throughout most of my adult life as I kept repeating the same behaviors that would only lead to more instability, more fear, and eventual abandonment. Until God! I only knew failure before Christ, before I became that highly favored child of God.

But even now, I realize I have been afraid of who I am in Him and the gifts He has given me. I have been afraid of success. Well, no more! I am claiming spiritual authority over my fear!

The Bible provides us with some examples of God's servants who also faced fear. I pray the following scriptures will be *Rhema* words in your own lives regarding your own fears.

In Jeremiah 1, the young prophet tried to make excuses and focused on his inadequacies. He was concerned over his youth, and that he may not have been eloquent. However, God was not accepting of Jeremiah's excuses.

God replied, "*Do not be afraid* of them, for I am with you and will rescue you." The King James Version translates it as "do not fear their faces."

God promises to be with us: "I will never leave you, or forsake you." His perfect love will cast out any fear you may have.

There is no room for excuses or self-doubt. You are a child of God! Walk in it!

No more excuses. If God gave you a job to do, He will provide you with everything you need to do it. However, the choice is yours.

When Jesus walked on the water, Jesus told them, *"Take courage! It is I . . . Do not be afraid."* (Matthew 14:27) Peter then took his walk on the water and was fine initially but then had to be snatched up by our Savior once he faltered and began to focus on other things.

It strikes me that Jesus did not let Peter fall. He won't let any of us fall either as long as we keep our focus centered on Christ.

God spoke to Abram when he was still Abram in Genesis 15:1. God said, *"Do not be afraid—I am your shield, your very great reward."* What have you been praying for that you are afraid to receive? What is your heart's desire? What great reward have you been promised? Why be afraid of your destiny? As you know, there is no room for double mindedness on these matters.

Psalms 138 is about God not abandoning the works of His hands. He will not abandon any of us. It also says the Lord will fulfill His purpose for me. He will fulfill his purpose for you.

Psalms 20:4 says, "May He give you the desire of your heart and make all your plans succeed." I think God wants us all in a place where we can be real with Him and with ourselves about our desires. He placed those desires there in the first place, and it is okay to hope for those things unseen, which have been promised, no matter how big or how small. God will grant the desires your heart.

Maybe you are afraid to believe, as I am at times, that God really can do it, whatever the "it" is in your life. You may have had past experiences that allowed you to only get so far in your dream, in your vision, in your calling, but there is no time to focus on yesterday's manna.

It is much easier not to walk in faith: "Well, God, you could but . . ." It would be so much easier not to walk in the calling. Many are called, few are chosen, and you have a choice. God may be choosing you, but what will you choose?

In Exodus 20:20—*"Do not be afraid,* God has come to test you, so that the fear of the Lord will be with you."—the context is, of course, after the Ten Commandments. The rest of the verse is "to keep you from sinning," but I still think it applies. Fear in this context also means reverence.

So I started to meditate on the dual meaning of the word: that emotion of dread and the complete reverence for our mighty God. I would encourage you to grab a hold of the reverence and let go of the dread.

In Genesis 32:9-12, where Jacob is preparing to meet Esau, he says, "Save me I pray . . . You have said, 'I will surely make you prosper.'" He prayed right through his fear, and he knew what God had promised and believed it.

In 1 Samuel 14:6, when Jonathan attacked the Philistines, he said to his armor bearer, "Come, let's go over to the outpost of those uncircumcised fellows. *Perhaps the Lord will act in our behalf. Nothing can hinder the Lord . . ."*

God will act in your behalf. Are you asking Him to? Nothing can hinder the plans He has for you. Are you trying to follow His plans or your own? Again, the choice is there for you to make.

You may fear that you have everything to lose (see Matthew 16:24-28), but you have everything to gain. Are you willing to pay the price? God will make a way if it is His will.

We all have issues that hinder us. There are physical, man-made, and spiritual walls—just like the walls of Jericho—that are in the way of our promise. You may think you have vast amounts of knowledge regarding the obstacles that lay before you, but God sees it all, and with God, *all* things really are possible!

God wants to do a miracle for you today. Have you asked?

So it is time . . . The choice is yours. Stop living in fear and lay hold of the promise that has been given to you!

HIS VERY OWN

You have established your people Israel as your very own forever, and you, O Lord, have become their God.

—2 Samuel 7:24

What about the one whom the Father set apart as his very own and sent into the world? Why then do you accuse me of blasphemy because I said, "I am God's Son?"

—John 10:36

Who gave Himself for us to redeem us from all wickedness and to purify for Himself a people that are his very own eager to do what is good.

—Titus 2:14

It happens to be Christmas Eve as I sit here and write this. My cats are here. Georgina is beside me, and Pumpkin is snuggled in by one of her toys, but it is very quiet. I can't hear any neighbors, TVs, music, or the outside world. This is one of the things I love most about this season in my life: the silence, the calm, the peace.

I'm not fretting over anything. I'm just here, content and contemplating the goodness of my Lord. I could pop in a DVD or a video, but not tonight and really not most nights either. No more rehearsing for Christmas, so no practice CD either. The only sound is my laptop fan, and the tap of my fingers on the keyboard.

I actually prefer to be in the quiet, by myself, alone physically, and yet I know that my God is with me. The significance of this moment is not lost on me.

For years, I made sure I was never alone as I've shared so many times; I filled my life with something or someone to make sure I would not have to deal with me. I chased the wind to exponential degrees. I can remember so many Solomon moments when I would realize that the men in my life were acting anything but lovingly toward me, and I just knew that to be loved and being in a loving relationship had to mean so much more than anything that I had. I remember so many nights crying myself to sleep, thinking, *This cannot be what love is.* Truth be told, I was the loneliest when I was involved in the supposedly deepest relationships.

The interesting thing about my life before Christ was that I rarely realized the extent of the mess I was in, and even if I did realize it, I did not have a clue on how to get out of it until I hit rock-bottom. But that is exactly where Jesus found me, and brought me up out of my mess, after I was finally ready to submit and admit that I was not able to solve my own problems. I knew that there was something better back then, but I didn't know what or how to find it.

God made a way for me to find Him. All it took was an invite from a coworker to come to a church service and the little seeds of truth that she planted. I was lost and hurting, and someone took the time to reach out and extend the love of Christ with that simple invite.

That coworker, who invited me to her church, would become a mentor, my spiritual mother, and a mother in almost every other way too. It is my prayer that no one ever underestimates the influence you may have on another person, or what God will grow from the seeds that you may plant. He will use the simple to confound the wise. Never feel inadequate when sharing your faith.

I once really was blind, and now I really can see. What He has done for me, He came to do for all mankind. He came to redeem us and set us free. He was born into this earthly world to eventually die for our sins.

So, I sit here tonight and look back at my rock-bottom, only to unpack more of the baggage from all those years. I can finally say I am alone but not lonely, and it is okay. I am okay only because of Jesus, His love, His mercy, and His grace. He really is Immanuel, God with us. He really is Jesus, the God who will save us.

God has really been speaking to my heart, during this Christmas season, that I am His very own, as are you, like in the scriptures above. The first is a part of a prayer from David, which I encourage you to read entirely. The scripture from John is obviously Jesus speaking. Paul's words to Titus still ring true in 2007.

I can finally say that I am loved, and I am in a loving relationship with God, a relationship so real—more real than anything I have ever known. I have found everything I was ever looking for. I am not lonely because I have God with me. Everyday is Christmas for me, and my salvation was the best gift I have ever received! Thank you, God! Remember, you are *His very own*!

———

HE WILL NEVER LET
THE RIGHTEOUS FALL

Psalms 55:22 says, "Cast your cares on the *Lord* and he will sustain you; he will never let the righteous fall."

I recently have found myself saying both parts of this scripture in different situations to different people and in different contexts, forgetting—in those particular moments—that scripturally they are both connected to one another. Today, this scripture found me, and that little semicolon connected the dots.

If I remember correctly from my grade-school grammar class, the semicolon is used to join two closely related thoughts instead of using a conjunction like *and*. So why care about a semicolon? After all, the book of Psalms was written long before the rules of modern grammar were designed. Furthermore, the book of Psalms was not even written in English to begin with, but someone, who was translating the original text back in the day of King James, felt that those two little sentences were close enough in meaning to link them with a semicolon.

When I had quoted that last part of the scripture to a dear saint—"He will never let the righteous fall"—I was more focusing on the idea that He would never leave us like in Hebrews, which references the Deuteronomy scripture:

> Keep your lives free from the love of money and be content with what you have, because God has said, "Never will I leave you; never will I forsake you." (Hebrews 13:5)

> Be strong and courageous. Do not be afraid or terrified because of them, for the *Lord* your God goes with you; he will never leave you nor forsake you. (Deuteronomy 31:6)

When I referenced the first part of the scripture to another individual, about casting your cares, I was more focusing on the overall theme in Psalm 55, which is our burdens are too heavy to carry alone—mostly too heavy to carry at all—and that Jehovah Jireh would provide. His burden is light, and His yoke is easy.

In Psalm 55:6, David was wishing for wings of a dove. How often would it be easier to just "fly away and be at rest"? However, God will make us lie down in green pastures, and He will give us rest in His time. He will sustain us with all that we need: strength, compassion, wisdom, knowledge, faith, love, joy, peace, and patience. He will provide for everything that will bring forth His purpose and plan for our lives—physically, emotionally, and spiritually.

I am always encouraged by Isaiah 40:31, which says, "But those who hope in the Lord will renew their strength. They will soar on wings like eagles; they will run and not grow weary, they will walk and not be faint."

Of course, Isaiah's eagle of strength is a little different than David's dove of escapism. I pray that all of you renew your strength and Hope in the Lord and soar like an eagle. Even if your flying feels initially like falling, you can cast your cares upon Him and know that He will sustain you, never allowing you to fall.

> Let us hold unswervingly to the hope we profess, for He who promised is faithful. (Hebrews 10:23)

THE COST

Uneasy lies the head that wears a crown.
—Shakespeare, *Henry IV* (part 2, act III, line 31)

King Henry IV is awake in the middle of the night and tortured by insomnia as he makes this comment about the burden that great responsibility can bring. He recognizes the cost of his position and authority.

To truly allow God to transform you and your life, there is also a cost. There is a cost to live and walk in your kingdom position and walk in the spiritual authority, which is your God-given right as a coheir.

> Then the mother of Zebedee's sons came to Him with her sons, kneeling down and asking something from Him. 21 And He said to her, "What do you wish?" She said to Him, "Grant that these two sons of mine may sit, one on your right hand and the other on the left, in your kingdom." 22 But Jesus answered and said, "You do not know what you ask. Are you able to drink the cup that I am about to drink, and be baptized with the baptism that I am baptized with?" They said to Him, "We are able." 23 So He said to them, "You will indeed drink My cup, and be baptized with the baptism that I am baptized with; but to sit on my right hand and on my left is not Mine to give, but it is for those for whom it is prepared by my Father." 24 And when the ten heard it, they were greatly displeased with the two brothers. 25 But Jesus called them to Himself and said, "You know that the rulers of the Gentiles lord it over them, and those who are great exercise authority over them. 26 Yet it shall not be so among you; but whoever desires to become great among you, let Him be your servant. 27 And whoever desires to be first among you, let Him be your slave—28 just as the Son of Man did not come

to be served, but to serve, and to give His life a ransom for many."
(Matthew 20:20-28, NKJV)

Jesus tells her that she has no idea what it is that she is really asking for. How often do we ask for things without first counting the cost?

James and John answer that they are able, proclaiming that they are willing to serve, suffer, and sacrifice along with Jesus. Can you really devote and invest what is needed for your prayer to be answered, for your heart's desire to become a reality, which most likely includes time, energy, self-discipline, and money?

How often do we have our own agenda of where we want to be? Allow the Father to place you into your kingdom position and place you where He wants you, where you will best be used for His purpose. Not everyone can be at the right or at the left, but know that He has a spot just for you that no one else can fill. No one else has lived your life or has your set of gifts and talents.

We wear a crown of grace only because our Savior first wore a crown of thorns. How can you be a better servant?

I Look Up

Keep My Eyes on You

GOD'S RAINBOW AND PEACE

Today I will make my way back to my old college stomping grounds. I have so many memories from living there.

The last time I went there was for a funeral, for my best friend M. It will be two years in a few days when she graduated into her heavenly, glorified, cancer-free body. She died several days before her thirty-fourth birthday. I recently donated twelve inches of my hair in her memory.

I was bound and determined to make sure that M would have her thirty-fourth birthday party regardless of her being in the hospital and, most certainly, regardless of the fact that she was dying.

I came bouncing into her hospital room in my usual hyperfashion with bags of gifts and cake and laughing and telling her that we just had to celebrate and spice up that boring old hospital wing. I was bubbling over with energy.

She was higher than the space shuttle on her IV pain meds, but I saw the joy in her eyes, looking at me and longing for some of the exuberance that I had. She knew her time was short, and so did I. That is the trouble sometimes with being a nurse because you just know things.

She was an incredible nurse. I had my babies in the NICU, and she had her adults in the ICU.

We were both experienced in death and the dying process, trained in it actually. We both had lots of hands-on experience, but it was always someone else experiencing the loss. It was never us.

She chose me to stay with her that last night that she was sort of "with it," not really able to talk too much but able to understand. It was an amazing night.

I sat awake with her, reliving stories of our past adventures and singing her songs, particularly that one we loved. It was the song with the video of a girl in the bumblebee outfit dancing around. We both loved it, and we used to listen to it on our way up to a local community college for Anatomy and Physiology II during nursing school. We played that song over and over and over and over again.

I sat in her hospital room, reminding her of some nursing school horrors, about different boys, parties that we used to attend, and of our West Virginia adventures. I reminded her about her wedding-day morning that we spent together getting our hair done. I was retelling our journey as friends.

Several days later, the call finally came just as expected. It didn't hurt any less. I remember the drive to her viewing more so than actually being there.

I was praying and driving and kept tearing up on and off. A few tears went trickling down my cheeks, and I wiped them away quickly. I was trying so hard to fight them back. I hate to cry.

I remember not long into the drive that there were these big billowy storm clouds, and the sky suddenly opened up and unleashed torrents. It was pounding sideways rain. My tears suddenly came pouring out as well, finally flooding my face, because I couldn't fight them off anymore; but around the bend in the road was a rainbow.

I couldn't stop looking at it. It was so beautiful with colors so vivid it didn't look real. Then, suddenly, my heart was filled with such peace. There was no more rain and no more tears, just that rainbow in the sky and an indescribable peace in my heart that surpassed my understanding.

There are only a few occasions in my life when I have seen rainbows, and they have all been very memorable and very purposefully placed for my viewing by our Creator. Can you remember, in your own life, the last time you saw a rainbow whether real or symbolic? Seen a manifestation of God's promise to you?

Of course, Noah automatically comes to mind when I think of rainbows. His story can be found in Genesis 6-9, and his is a story of faith, hope, and a promise.

> God said, "Whenever I bring clouds over the earth and the rainbow appears in the clouds, I will remember my covenant between me and you . . ." (Genesis 9:14-15, NIV)

Even through the storms in our lives, He knows that His rainbow is right around the bend; but like Noah, we've got to do our part. We must build the ark and move in faith in Him. He will take care of the details.

Keep Your Eyes Fixed on Jesus

Let us fix our eyes on Jesus, the author and perfecter of our faith, who
for the joy set before Him endured the cross, scorning its shame, and
sat down at the right hand of the throne of God.
—Hebrews 12:2, NIV (emphasis added)

Our eyes need to be fixed on Jesus, not on circumstances, not on other
people's judgments about us, not on other's expectations of us, not on our
situations, and not focused on how we feel or how we think things should be.
How easy is it to lose hope sometimes because things do not turn out the way
you want or you feel passed over or find out the way someone really feels about
you? The devil would try to make you doubt God and your own self-worth. He
does seek to devour you. That is why our armor needs to be on at all times.

I was struck by the fact that the scripture says Jesus is the author. He is not
just an object of our faith. The word *author* implies action and motion. He is
creating our faith actively.

Then the scripture continues with saying that Jesus is not only the author of
our faith, but also the *perfecter.* He is making your faith perfect. So is the current
circumstance in motion in your life so that your faith can be perfected?

Hebrews 11:1 (NIV) says, "Now faith is being *sure* of what we hope for
and *certain* of what we do not see." Sure and certain. So if our eyes are fixed on
Jesus, we can remain sure and certain that God is working out His plan in our
lives no matter what our human eyes see, what our human hearts feel, or what
our earthly brains think.

Give to Caesar What Is Caesar's, Give to God What Is God's

Then the Pharisees went out and laid plans to trap Him in His words. They sent their disciples to Him along with the Herodians. "Teacher," they said, "we know you are a man of integrity and that you teach the way of God in accordance with the truth. You aren't swayed by men, because you pay no attention to who they are. Tell us then, what is your opinion? Is it right to pay taxes to Caesar or not?" But Jesus, knowing their evil intent, said, "You hypocrites, why are you trying to trap me? Show me the coin used for paying the tax." They brought Him a denarius, and He asked them, "Whose portrait is this? And whose inscription?" "Caesar's," they replied. Then He said to them, "Give to Caesar what is Caesar's, and to God what is God's." When they heard this, they were amazed. So they left Him and went away.

—Matthew 22:15-22

Jesus did not get into some great debate over Roman taxes or discuss each group's politics (Pharisees vs. Herodians, Democrats vs. Republican, red state vs. blue state), but He certainly did use their scheme to teach us about money. Jesus says, in this scripture, to "give to Caesar what is Caesar's, and to God what is God's." During this time of year, tax season, giving to the US government, our Caesar, always becomes a focus for all citizens.

In years past, I would often get upset about how high my taxes were and how much of my income the government was actually taking. I always thought, *If I could just have what I made for one paycheck, I could catch up.* Coupled with this were my poor past and sinful choices that left my finances in ruin. I was always angry and blaming my past mistakes for what my present looked like.

Add to this anger a bank account that never seemed to have enough money, which only continued the cycle of using more credit, which was a scheme straight out of the evil pit of hell. I thought I was robbing Peter to pay Paul. Really, I was robbing God of what I owed Him.

I will share that, for the first couple of years of my walk, I did not always give to God what was God's. Until one day, a few months ago, a scripture was read that dealt with tithing, and it would not leave me alone. The Word rang in my ears over and over like an audio loop, a record that kept playing. There came a moment that I realized I was being disobedient, and that it had nothing to do with money and everything due to my lack of trust, of faith, that God would provide.

Through a discussion with my spiritual father, God revealed that I had to take the step out of the boat in faith. I needed to stop using the credit cards, start giving the full 10 percent of what I earned not just what my take-home pay was, and I should test and see just like the Word says. Ouch! The truth hurts sometimes, but I believe God gives us people in our lives to tell us things that we need to hear not what we want to hear.

So test and see I did—no more credit card use and no more 10 percent of my take-home pay. I was out of the boat and felt like I was drowning.

Shortly after Christmas, one Thursday night, I was almost out of gas, and I was nervous because I was not sure if I would have enough gas to last me until Monday's payday. I was calculating in my mind how many times I would have to drive out to the church, back home, to work, back to church . . . then my miracle. Jehovah Jireh provided!

A sweet sister in Christ handed me an envelope with a $10 bill inside of it for leading sectionals over the Christmas season to help prepare for the concert. The tears rose up. I told her my empty gas-tank worries and thanked her and then thanked God.

Now I am a cheerful giver, not out of obligation but out of reverence and obedience. He wants obedience above sacrifice. Now I'm no longer angry and resentful over what mere mortal men decide to take from my paycheck whether they are Democrat or Republican. Let Caesar take from my pay whatever he wants because he is not in control. Let the Republicans and Democrats spew their presidential promises, and the political analysts make their projections about who will do what to our taxes. None of them are in control.

Now I'm looking up toward heaven and not looking back anymore and being continually shamed, feeling guilty over my past financial mistakes. There is liberty and freedom in Christ. My sister called me last night about my taxes for this year, and I will share that I am getting a return greater than any in all of my working life except for the year I was married. I asked her why, and she told me that it was my tithes that made the difference.

Focus

"Therefore, since we are surrounded by such a great cloud of witnesses, let us throw off everything that hinders and the sin that so easily entangles, and let us run with perseverance the race marked out for us. Let us fix our eyes on Jesus, the author and perfecter of our faith, who for the joy set before Him endured the cross, scorning its shame, and sat down at the right hand of the throne of God. Consider Him who endured such opposition from sinful men, so that you will not grow weary and lose heart. In your struggle against sin, you have not yet resisted to the point of shedding your blood. And you have forgotten that word of encouragement that addresses you as sons: "My son, do not make light of the Lord's discipline, and do not lose heart when he rebukes you, because the Lord disciplines those he loves, and he punishes everyone he accepts as a son." Endure hardship as discipline; God is treating you as sons. For what son is not disciplined by his father? If you are not disciplined [and everyone undergoes discipline], then you are illegitimate children and not true sons. Moreover, we have all had human fathers who disciplined us and we respected them for it. How much more should we submit to the Father of our spirits and live! Our fathers disciplined us for a little while as they thought best; but God disciplines us for our good, that we may share in his holiness. No discipline seems pleasant at the time, but painful. Later on, however, it produces a harvest of righteousness and peace for those who have been trained by it. Therefore, strengthen your feeble arms and weak knees. "Make level paths for your feet," so that the lame may not be disabled, but rather healed."

—Hebrews 12:1-13

Have you been hindered recently, entangled not just by sin but by life's circumstances? Tired of running the race that seems to never end? Where's your focus? Are your eyes fixed upon Jesus?

The scripture says to "endure hardship," "submit to the Father," and "run with perseverance." Stay focused, not on the hardship or pain, but on Jesus. Let the hardship train you so it may produce a harvest of righteousness and peace.

Feeling so run-down and run over by life that you have wobbly, weak knees? Have your arms ever been so tired that you feel feeble? Strengthen yourself with the power of the Spirit, with the Bread of Life, with the Living Word. He is the sustainer of your soul.

The encouragement in Hebrews echoes Proverbs 4:26: "Make level paths for your feet and take only ways that are firm." Verse 27 continues with "do not swerve to the right or the left; keep your foot from evil."

There have been many times when I have had wobbly knees in my walk thus far, and many times that I have been so consumed with the circumstances that I was unable to see what was really going on. My life became so out of focus that I was not able to clearly see where God was trying to lead me.

Most recently, ministry activities became my focus. I was serving and serving, pouring out all that I had every week. While I found God through the music, there came a time when He seemed hidden from me. It was a fight and battle to get into the presence of the Almighty. Suddenly, it felt like my world was crumbling. I was not my normal self. I was becoming resentful about having to attend scheduled practices and almost never practiced anytime outside of that.

The decisions I needed to make did not make sense to me, but they made perfect sense in God's plan. I was so focused on what was going on around me, feeling that I had to continue to serve in that way, that I was actually hindering myself. How many of you know that God will allow you to keep going until you get to the end of yourself?

I kept serving at an impossible level, and it felt like painful torture to every fiber of my being, and it was on display for all to see every Sunday for three services. I thought enduring the hardship meant that I needed to continue the path that I had been walking when God simply wanted me to walk away.

He had already shown me the level path, yet I refused to take it because it did not make sense to me. He had already revealed that I was to be concentrating on Him first then these devotionals and the original music.

I was so concerned about everyone else's needs in the ministry that I had neglected my own. Second Thessalonians 3:13 says, "And as for you, brothers, never tire of doing what is right." I thought it was right to remain, but that would have been very wrong.

———

Stepping out of the fray felt like eight billion tons had been lifted off my shoulders. It was a tearful conversation with the leadership, but very encouraging at the same time, because I knew I was finally being obedient to what God had already said.

Be encouraged today! Stay focused!

PILATE POLITICS

Now Jesus stood before the governor. And the governor asked Him, saying, "Are You the King of the Jews?" So Jesus said to him, "It is as you say." And while He was being accused by the chief priests and elders, He answered nothing.

Then Pilate said to Him, "Do You not hear how many things they testify against You?" But He answered him not one word, so that the governor marveled greatly.

Now at the feast the governor was accustomed to releasing to the multitude one prisoner whom they wished. And at that time they had a notorious prisoner called Barabbas. Therefore, when they had gathered together, Pilate said to them, "Whom do you want me to release to you? Barabbas, or Jesus who is called Christ?" For he knew that they had handed Him over because of envy. While he was sitting on the judgment seat, his wife sent to him, saying, "Have nothing to do with that just Man, for I have suffered many things today in a dream because of Him."

But the chief priests and elders persuaded the multitudes that they should ask for Barabbas and destroy Jesus. The governor answered and said to them, "Which of the two do you want me to release to you?" They said, "Barabbas!" Pilate said to them, "What then shall I do with Jesus who is called Christ?" They all said to him, "Let Him be crucified!"

Then the governor said, "Why, what evil has He done?" But they cried out all the more, saying, "Let Him be crucified!" When Pilate saw that he could not prevail at all, but rather that a tumult was rising, he took water and washed his hands before the multitude, saying, "I am innocent of the blood of this just Person. You see to it."

And all the people answered and said, "His blood be on us and on our children." Then he released Barabbas to them; and when he had scourged Jesus, he delivered Him to be crucified.
—Matthew 27:11-26, NKJV

Debates, e-mails, lunch conversations, T-shirts, buttons, comedy skits, speaking in tongues . . . politics! It seems to be everywhere right now, and I don't even have cable here at the crib. It is perhaps one of the most divisive things presently running rampant through this country with the elections only a few weeks away. The evil one is busy for sure.

Who is tired of the propaganda, the quotes and sound bites taken out of context, the mudslinging attacks, and the e-mails? I certainly am and have had about enough of the media circus that this election, in particular, has become especially in cyberspace.

I really encourage everyone to pray for our nation, no matter who you plan on voting for or which one wins, because this election is about way more than just one man taking office. Repent, for the time, is at hand! (see Matthew 4:17) I believe our focus needs to be on God and our Savior particularly at this time.

I love in Luke 8:25 where it says ". . . He commands even the winds and water, and they obey Him." Now there is a campaign promise you won't hear from either side. I don't think either candidate brought streams out of a rocky crag and made water flow down like rivers (Psalms 78:16). They are both just mere mortal men.

I came to the realization today, at work, as I watched the stock market plummet to the lowest levels I've ever seen it since I started paying attention to it—that our forefathers put "in God we trust" on our money because they knew that the money is not where our trust belongs and where most people put it. Just as our trust does not belong in man. Those words serve as a constant reminder of the fact that our focus needs to be upward, not on man or political candidates and certainly not on money or stocks.

I used to love to get into philosophical debates, heated political discussions, and the like. Now I really won't do either. If you really meditate upon the above scripture in Matthew, that whole section, you will see time and time again that Pilate had a choice to do the right thing, which is seldom the easy thing. He had a choice to please the crowd, ensuring his political future, or go against his constituents. You will also note the response of Jesus who also had a choice and, yet, did not respond to even a single charge. He knew who He was, and that He did not have to.

Of course, there will be people reading this from both sides of the aisle and I love all God's people no matter if you are a Republican, an Independent, or a Democrat. We all have choices to make on election day as we must exercise our right of enfranchisement. I pray for all of you that doing the right thing is more important than the politics of man as you push the button on November 4. Allow God to lead you as you make your choices.

Remember that God loves you most, cares about you most, and makes promises that you can count on. Let Him guide you in all decisions.

His Rainbows, His Covenants, His Promises!

We first see covenant mentioned in the Bible (NIV, NKJV, and KJV) in relation to Noah in Genesis 6:18, which reads, "But I will establish my covenant with you, and you will enter the ark—you and your sons and your wife and your sons' wives with you." Then we find the connection, and link is made between the covenant and the rainbow.

> And God said, "This is the sign of the covenant I am making between me and you and every living creature with you, a covenant for all generations to come: 13 I have set my rainbow in the clouds, and it will be the sign of the covenant between me and the earth. 14 Whenever I bring clouds over the earth and the rainbow appears in the clouds, 15 I will remember my covenant between me and you and all living creatures of every kind. Never again will the waters become a flood to destroy all life. 16 Whenever the rainbow appears in the clouds, I will see it and remember the everlasting covenant between God and all living creatures of every kind on the earth." 17 So God said to Noah, "This is the sign of the covenant I have established between me and all life on the earth." (Genesis 9:12-17)

There are hundreds of references for the word *covenant* in the whole Bible (NIV), according to my search on a popular Christian Web site. The Bible dictionaries and commentaries all have tons of definitions and supporting scriptures. See Deuteronomy 4:31, Psalms 89:3, Psalms 105:8-11, Hebrews 6:13-20, Luke 1:68-75, Isaiah 59:21, and Jeremiah 31:33, 31:34 for a quick study.

In contrast, if you search for the word *rainbow*, you only find it six times of which three are in connection with the covenant. The other three are below:

> Like the appearance of a rainbow in the clouds on a rainy day, so was the radiance around Him. This was the appearance of the likeness of the glory of the Lord. When I saw it, I fell facedown, and I heard the voice of one speaking. (Ezekiel 1:28)

> And the one who sat there had the appearance of jasper and carnelian. A rainbow, resembling an emerald, encircled the throne. (Revelations 4:3)

> Then I saw another mighty angel coming down from heaven. He was robed in a cloud, with a rainbow above his head; his face was like the sun, and his legs were like fiery pillars. (Revelations 10:1)

I encourage you to think back the last time you saw a rainbow. Meditate upon the promises that God has given to you and ponder on all the ways God had shown His divine faithfulness to you. What has God promised you specifically? What covenant is God making with you, and what promise are you making to Him?

My prayer for all of you is from Hebrews 13:20-21

> May the God of peace, who through the blood of the eternal covenant brought back from the dead our Lord Jesus, that great Shepherd of the sheep, equip you with everything good for doing His will, and may he work in us what is pleasing to Him, through Jesus Christ, to whom be glory for ever and ever. Amen.

Remember to keep looking up whether it's raining or sunny outside. Otherwise, you will never see your rainbow!

I Stand in Awe

How Can They Not Believe

THE JEWELS SMUSH

Right after high school, I started attending a local university as a vocal performance major and was being classically trained as a mezzo-soprano. I smoked and partied my way through the music program for about a year and a half. I learned many things like how to conduct, in one time signature with one hand and, in a completely different time signature with the other hand. I learned how to fake my way through a whole year of piano including improvising and everything having to do with my left hand.

To say that my current piano skills are weak is an understatement, and I actually would not even consider myself to have any skill at all. However, there have been a few times that I can remember, since February of 2006, when God began filling my head with melodies, harmonies, symphonies, lyrics, and horn lines seemingly out of the blue that I approached my electronic keyboard to perform the Jewels Smush. This technique was never taught in my music program—just so everything is clear.

It is very simple, and you need no musical knowledge to understand it. The Jewels Smush is simply this:

1. You approach the piano or keyboard and proceed to press down as many keys as you can all at the same time—not necessarily aggressively either.
2. The quantity of tones is the point of it all. The more notes, the better! Your whole arm works nicely. Both arms produce the best results.
3. The sustain pedal must be depressed. That way, what you are left with is a big conglomeration of mess, dissonance, musical disorder, chaos, and a not-so-lovely sound.

I was explaining this technique to a pianist who writes music, and I offered it as a suggestion as she was explaining her occasional frustration with song writing, like when you don't know where to go with the song or piece you are composing. I'm sure you can imagine the look I got.

So I proceeded to explain further, explaining part of my testimony with regard to God's amazing gift of song. Song writing, apparently, does not happen the same way for everyone, which I am just now beginning to realize. I guess some people write songs all the way through their lives from childhood up into adulthood.

For me, it all started very suddenly and seemingly out of the blue about a year and a half ago. There was a time once before, but that is for another day. I know that I am only a vessel, so it is an indescribable thing for me sometimes to listen back on my digital voice recorder to what flows out of me, but to God be all the glory.

Sometimes the words and melody come together all at the same time. I can't write fast enough or get to my digital voice recorder quickly enough. Sometimes, in my head, I hear just a melody, with a few notes, or a phrase that takes off and erupts. Other times, there have been instruments playing like a muted horn, a piano, and a sax. Still other times, there have been all the different vocal parts laid out exactly how they should be layered and blended together—voices. Sometimes I only get an outpouring of words, which really are my prayers written down or just a chorus. There have been times where the parts come separately on different days, weeks, or months—a verse here, a bridge there, or a chorus.

In general, I try to stay away from the keyboard that sits here in my living room unless I am practicing someone else's music, a singular line with my right hand only. I once tried to put chords to a melody, and when I was done making a mess of it, it no longer fit together the way I had heard it in my head originally. I was very nicely and gently told, after I shared that mess with my musical mentor, not to change the way I write. I understood the comment and learned the lesson, but I fully recognized also that it really was not me doing the writing to start with.

Sometimes I wish my hands could do what is in my head, but God has not ordained it that way, and I learned that, if I try to do it within myself, I will make a mess of it! I could spend the rest of my life praying, writing, and repenting on just that topic: learning how to be totally dependent on God and how to stop trying to fix things myself.

So the few times that I used "The Smush" were before my failed attempt at trying to chord out a song. I could relate to that frustration that the pianist above was describing. Not knowing what is next can be a terrible place to be.

I remember sitting down and doing steps 1-3 as listed above, and what came out of it was God's answer . . . That one tone, that hum that stuck out, that one note that fit. How often is life like that? We question, "Where do I go, God? What's next? Where and what would you have me do? Why?"

Sometimes life feels like the Smush—messy, chaotic, and out of sync—but if we go to God, He will provide the answer.

I pray that each of you—those of you who know Christ and those who do not in your own life, in your own walk, in facing your own challenges, and in going through life's peaks and valleys—are encouraged by Psalm 20:1-8 (NIV):

> May the Lord answer you when you are in distress; may the name of the God of Jacob protect you. May he send you help from the sanctuary and grant you support from Zion. May he remember all your sacrifices and accept your burnt offerings. Selah

> May he give you the desire of your heart and make all your plans succeed. We will shout for joy when you are victorious and will lift up our banners in the name of our God. May the Lord grant all your requests. Now I know that the Lord saves his anointed; he answers him from his holy heaven with the saving power of his right hand. Some trust in chariots and some in horses, but we trust in the name of the Lord our God. They are brought to their knees and fall, but we rise up and stand firm.

1630

That's what I heard, *1630,* which woke me up early one Wednesday morning. The clock said 4:07 AM, and I was so tired, exhausted really. I had been in a faith crisis of sorts just hours before I finally fell asleep. I had sought solace in Matthew in the midst of my wrestling. So I thought maybe it was Matthew 16:30. I filled in the blank.

So up and out of bed I went and began flipping through the pages, wondering if it was Matthew 16:30. I found where it should be.

> 24 Then Jesus said to his disciples, "If anyone would come after me, he must deny Himself and take up his cross and follow me. 25 For whoever wants to save his life will lose it, but whoever loses his life for me will find it. 26 What good will it be for a man if he gains the whole world, yet forfeits his soul? Or what can a man give in exchange for his soul? 27 For the Son of Man is going to come in his Father's glory with his angels, and then he will reward each person according to what he has done. 28 I tell you the truth, some who are standing here will not taste death before they see the Son of Man coming in his kingdom." (Matthew 16:24-28)

Thus began my middle-of-the night conversation with God. "Okay, take up my cross and lose my life, but no verse 30, God." So I started thinking I was really crazy and losing my mind, but the chapter after that, in Matthew 17, is where the transfiguration is. This caught my eye since I had just done a gem devotional on that. "Okay—sorry, God—guess I should not fill in Your blanks!"

I still had this lingering thought on what 1630 was, with no answer. Wednesday came and went filled with more wrestling and more battling. I wanted to sleep desperately but could not.

Thursday, it was very early in the morning when I heard again that voice saying, "1630." I popped out of bed like a firecracker had gone off. "What is 1630?" I began my pacing, talking to God, frustrated, and wrestling. I made my way to my Bible once again and was flipping through the pages, ready to flip out.

I was turning and turning, looking at lyrics and notes page after page, and it came to me. Finally, my answer was revealed. I quickly found *PAGE 1630*. It was not marked or flagged with anything with no writing, no marker, no highlighter—nothing.

The first couple of verses were the end of the Transfiguration in Mark 9, which parallels Matthew 17 that I had looked at the night before. I recognized the text, and then like a neon sign, verse 23 lights up. "Everything is possible for him who believes." There it was—the answer to all my battling, my unbelief.

So of course, the tears came. It was as if God wanted to remind me that He really is Jehovah Shammah, the God who is there, that He really is El Roi, the God who sees me. *He* hears every word when I cry out, and He saves every tear I cry in that bottle.

What an exhausting process! Off to work I went. I was tired and barely able to open my eyes. I was praying for God to take me through the rest of the day without falling over from lack of sleep.

At my desk, I have a calendar that has scriptures for every week on Sunday. I had not read the verse for that week yet, so I sleepily looked at it to cross off the prior day, and there was another Word waiting to remind me. Again, like a neon sign and just like the Bethlehem star, that verse lit my day. Micah 7:7 reads, "But as for me, I watch in hope for the Lord, I wait for God my Savior; my God will hear me."

So there was more confirmation in God's Word waiting for me to see it. It was there the whole time, just as He is there all the time, waiting for me to see Him, to hear Him, and to know Him and waiting for me to lift my arms in submission and call out "Abba, Father." He is waiting for me to really believe that all things are possible with Him.

Be blessed and be encouraged and know that God really does hear you and see you. He knows *all* about you. He *cares* for you, and He loves you. He knows every bit of pain you have endured and will make you whole.

BE SURE

Not everyone who says to me, "Lord, Lord," will enter the kingdom of heaven, but only he who does the will of my Father who is in heaven. 22 Many will say to me on that day, "Lord, Lord, did we not prophesy in your name, and in your name drive out demons and perform many miracles?" 23 Then I will tell them plainly, "I never knew you. Away from me, you evildoers!" 24 Therefore everyone who hears these words of mine and puts them into practice is like a wise man who built his house on the rock.

—Matthew 7:21-24, NIV

Every time I hear or come across this bit of scripture, it causes me to stop because of the little part, right at the beginning in verse 21 that is so important. I know a lot of people who say they believe, but there is a crucial next step beyond belief. It involves doing the "will of the Father" and putting the words into practice.

Can you BE SURE you will enter the kingdom of heaven?

B = Believe. Do you believe that Jesus was the Son of God sent to die in

E = Exchange for your sins?

SU = Submit. Are you able to submit your life to Him? In all ways, are you able to let go of your will, your agenda, and your plans?

RE = Restoration. Are you able to let Him change your life, your mind, and your heart so that He can restore you?

Are you sure you will spend eternity in heaven after your earthly body dies? What do you trust in? What are you committed to? What do you delight yourself in?

CHOICES

He has shaped each person in turn; now he watches everything
we do.
—Psalm 33:15 (Message)

Life and the choices we make sometimes leads us to places we do not
understand, but I love the way The Message translates this verse. He has shaped
each person, and He watches everything we do—everything.

This is my last gem from apartment 609. I think about the before-Christ
choices that brought me here to this space. I had sold my house, and my now
ex-husband was in jail. I was just really starting my walk with God. I was a
baby Christian, embryonic really. I was not involved in ministry three years ago
and never thought I would sing again though the idea was starting to blossom
in my brain. But life was still all about me and what I wanted, and I was still
holding myself back.

I was so hopeful, when I moved here, that somehow things would be
different, never realizing the journey God would lead me on while I was here
and, oh, what a journey it has been.

Packing has caused me to unpack a whole lot, and I have come to the realization
that it is only because of God that we can change at all. Changing my address
changed nothing about my life three years ago, but God has changed everything
about me since. However, this has been partly my choice. Surrendering one's will
is not an easy task, and it has been and continues to be quite a process.

I still have struggles and actually, the deeper my walk goes, the more those
struggles seem to intensify. Sometimes, in my God space, I cry out "Lord, I
believe! Help my unbelief!" and proclaim that I will "live by faith and not by
sight!" Now those are truly challenging to live out when faced with issues in
real life. It is so easy to speak scripture but so hard to make Godly choices and
really live by it.

—

Before finding my way back to God, I made a choice to say "I do" and enter into the bonds of matrimony. I found a Valentine's Day card, while packing, from the ex with a picture of us on our wedding day by the park bench at the museum. We looked so happy, but what it looked like was not the reality. What things appear to be are not always what things truly are, which is why God needs to define the truth in every situation and be the foundation for every choice we make.

I look back over the past three years and can see how God has used each situation to shape me, all the while watching me and watching to see what decisions I have made. I pray that I have made Him smile more than a few times and thank Him that He continually keeps those new mercies coming, morning after morning, because I need them more than ever.

Recently, there have been numerous reminders that it doesn't matter what you say but, rather, how you live and what choices you make in this life. Those reminders came from both saved and unsaved friends. I'm listening, God.

With the close of this season at 609 comes the acknowledgment of what God has done in my life as I look back and the excitement of what lies ahead and how God will use the next phase in my journey to continue to shape me and mold me. I know His eyes will be watching me, seeing every choice I make!

So as I sign off from 609, just know that God does love you most! He is watching!

Mary Christmas

At Christmas, Mary seems to come to the forefront in many different ways even to nonreligious or nonbelieving people. She is on pictures and cards and in manger scenes, and even the average person walking down the street knows her name.

My Catholic background made her name roll off my tongue so many times, but she still was never a real person to me. We prayed the Hail Mary all the time, which is basically what Gabriel said to her (Luke 1:28), followed by what Elizabeth spoke to her when Mary went to visit (Luke 1:42). I never even knew that part of the prayer was scripture when I was a practicing Catholic.

For those who are not Catholic, the prayer is as follows:

> Hail Mary, full of grace, the Lord is with thee [Gabriel's words to Mary]. Blessed are you among women, and blessed is the fruit of thy womb, Jesus [Elizabeth's words]. [Elizabeth does not say this next part. It was added around the end of the fifteenth century and then became part of the prayer.] Holy Mary, Mother of God, pray for us sinners, now, and at the hour of our death. Amen.

I could never be an advocate for religion now that I have a relationship, and I'm not placing more importance on Mary than I am on the birth of our Lord and Savior, but I do think there are some important things we can learn from this very real, very important person.

As you read through Luke's recounting of the birth of our Savior, I get the sense that Mary was just a simple peasant girl and maybe nothing notable or outstanding to those around her. She wasn't some princess in a palace, from some famous family of the time, with servants and fancy clothes. She was not on the front page of the society section of *The Jerusalem Times*. She was just a girl in a little village, going about her daily life.

When the angel Gabriel appears to her, he calls her highly favored and says that the Lord is with her. Of course, then he tells her not to be afraid and tells her again that she has found favor with God, that she will give birth to the Son of the Most High, that He will reign forever, and that His kingdom will have no end.

We could stop right there and ponder that for days. God's favor did not put her in a palace overnight. In fact, God's favor would come at a very great personal cost to her. In the short-term, she had to deal with the stigma of a pregnancy before marriage. Can you imagine the scandal in Nazareth, and how Mary and Joseph must have been the talk of the town? She could have been killed for that pregnancy.

Can you really imagine telling your soon-to-be-husband and parents that an angel told you that you would bear the Son of God? That conversation, I'm sure, left her parents and Joseph with some raised eyebrows.

Gabriel tells her how she will become pregnant and tells her about Elizabeth's pregnancy when Mary knows that Elizabeth is too old to bear a child. I love that Gabriel announces that *nothing is impossible with God,* in verse 37, after she questions him on how she could possibly give birth since she was a virgin. She then replies to Gabriel, "I am the Lord's servant . . . May it be to me as you have said." Talk about faith and submission!

She did not reply with doubt, and she did not question it. She seems to willingly accept what seems so humanly impossible.

Mary's song of praise, The Magnificat, has been made into so many different musical expressions, made famous by Bach, Pachelbel, and Vivaldi just to name a few. *Magnificat* is Latin for *magnifies* as Mary sings out "My soul doth magnify the Lord" in response to Elizabeth's words (Luke 1:42-45).

I have often pondered this bit of scripture as I have repeated it countless times during my own worship and times of prayer. To magnify means to make larger, and in the words of John the Baptist, Elizabeth's son, *"He must increase, but I must decrease"* (John 3:30, KJV).

Mary's song of praise continues with acknowledging the gift that God has given her and she praises God for who He is. We know how her son's life would end and the unimaginable pain that she will face, but we also know the hope for all mankind that she will carry and birth.

I pray for all of you that Christmas is a celebration of the birth of our Lord, Savior, and Redeemer. I pray that it is a time when you are able to have renewed faith and submit to God's plans for you as we get ready to enter into a new year. I pray that you are able to believe that nothing is impossible with God, and that everything about your life and your very being magnifies the Lord. I pray that you are able to acknowledge God's special gift to you, and above all, that you are able to praise Him for who He is.

—

He must increase, but I must decrease. (John 3:30, KJV)

The bride belongs to the bridegroom. The friend who attends the bridegroom waits and listens for Him, and is full of joy when he hears the bridegroom's voice. That joy is mine, and it is now complete. 30 He must become greater; I must become less. 31 The one who comes from above is above all; the one who is from the earth belongs to the earth, and speaks as one from the earth. The one who comes from heaven is above all. 32 He testifies to what he has seen and heard, but no one accepts his testimony. 33 The man who has accepted it has certified that God is truthful. 34 For the one whom God has sent speaks the words of God, for God gives the Spirit without limit. 35 The Father loves the Son and has placed everything in his hands. 36 Whoever believes in the Son has eternal life, but whoever rejects the Son will not see life, for God's wrath remains on Him. (John 3:29-36, NIV)

WAIT AND WATCH

But as for me, I watch in hope for the Lord, I wait for God my Savior; my God will hear me.

—Micah 7:7

During this time of prayer and fasting, some interesting things have happened over here at 609, things that let me know that God is really hearing me. It is Tuesday night, and I was not planning on going over to the church for the corporate prayer time. I was going to stay here and have my usual alone time with God in prayer and worship. Tonight was dedicated and consecrated to a very specific thing. I had started here alone at 609 and then felt that gentle nudge that I should head over to the church. So I did.

I began praying there just as I did at 609, and then God sent someone to pray over me. It was an amazing God moment. It never ceases to amaze me when God sends people, who don't know anything about you, to speak life into you and speak about specific things that no one else knows about except you and God.

I stopped on the way home for gas in my woozy spiritual state, and I accidentally got gas on my glove, so I came home and threw the pair into the wash. I started going through my coat pockets to wash that as well and found a piece of paper that had something written on it—Micah 7:7—the scripture above. I don't remember writing it nor do I know how long it has been in my jacket. So when I looked it up, I was so encouraged and blessed.

I send the events of my evening along only to encourage those of you who may feel like God isn't listening to you, that He's not real, or that He does not care about you, because those are just lies from the enemy. I encourage you all to be watchful. Watch for God to move in your life in your everyday activities. Not all of us get burning bushes and angel visitations, but watch for Him. He's watching you. He knew exactly what I needed to hear tonight. He knew that there was a piece of paper in my pocket with that scripture on it. He knew I would get gas on my glove and be cleaning out my pockets tonight.

I encourage all of you to keep waiting for the Lord—wait for His timing, His purpose, His plans, and His will. Before this fast began, I thought I was so yielded to all those things, but God has revealed how I was still hanging on in certain areas of my life. The waiting game is hard, and there is nothing easy about it, any of it. I never knew I was so willful, and letting God work that out is definitely a process that I know I must journey through.

However, I take great comfort in knowing that I am not alone in my journey. I know that He hears me, sees me, and loves me every step of the way.

Whatever you are going through today, just know that you are not alone. Even if you don't believe, He's waiting with open arms! Reach for Him and call upon Him!

THE PERFECTLY IMPERFECT STORM

My lease renewal notice arrived out of the blue. What was so unexpected about this renewal was the amount of the increase in my monthly rent should I choose to re-up. Last year, nothing came at all. They must have missed me (Thank you, Lord), but they were going to make up for that. The amount of the increase may as well have been a billion dollars. It threw me into such a tailspin I can't even put it into words. However, it would be the perfect storm in my imperfect life for God to reveal Himself.

> Jesus was in the stern, sleeping on a cushion. The disciples woke Him and said to Him, "Teacher, don't you care if we drown?" He got up, rebuked the wind and said to the waves "Quiet! Be Still!" The wind died down and it was completely calm. He said to the disciples "Why are you so afraid? Do you still have no faith?" (Mark 4:38-40)

Like Peter and the rest of the apostles in the boat, in Mark 4, with the sea tossing them to and fro like they were stuck in the middle of the storm of the century, I too ran to my Savior in a panic, in a state of internal chaos. My mind was racing with the internal calculator cha-chinging overtime, calculating the cost to stay versus leaving my humble abode. Sheer terror was running rampant. I was crying out, "GOD, EMERGENCY, ALERT, CODE PANIC. God please report to 609, STAT! They are going to jack up the rent, God. WHAT am I going to do? How will I ever be able to do this? I'm all alone! There is no one to help me move all this stuff! I cannot pick up the couch by myself!"

It was the chaos of a crisis and what I was always used to in life before God. It is funny how easy it was to slip back into that mess and the old thought processes: me, I, me, me, I, I, and me. It was all about me. Forgive me, Lord.

Instead, I should have been reaching out, pleading, "God, I'm having a self-centered focus problem. Please divert my attention away from me and onto

You!" But in the midst, I couldn't even see it for what it was. Then, to top it off, I became very ill and felt more miserable than I ever had before.

I leapt into action despite not being able to breathe, fevering, and generally feeling like a truck had hit me going about 209 miles per hour. I visited four complexes, did three drive-bys, and made one call. No deal! I found big security deposits, pet deposits, waiting lists, etc. The more I scurried around, the worse and more scared I felt.

At one point, I was so overwhelmed and exhausted that the tears poured forth like Niagara despite my scripture quoting. I was proclaiming, with a holy boldness, Mark 9:24, "I do believe, help my unbelief," and verse 23, "Everything is possible for Him who believes." I was rebuking the fear with 1 John 4:18—"Perfect love drives out fear"—and 2 Timothy 1:7, which says, "God did not give us a spirit of timidity, but a spirit power, of love, and of self-discipline."

The initial chaotic confusion eventually turned into plans of eating at the soup kitchen and walking everywhere due to lack of money for gas. Once I sat down and did a yearly cost projection, it was less expensive for me to stay here and suck up the overwhelming increase.

Sometimes, I wonder if God just watches me and scratches His head and says, "Hello? When are you going to get it, Jewels?" In His infinite wisdom and patience, He waited for me yet again.

Once I quieted myself before the Lord, it was like Jesus Himself called out peace and be still. And then God . . . two rainless rainbows later, I finally got it.

It was the last complex I planned on visiting before giving up totally even though I was resigned to being defeated. I was actually driving away after having wasted twenty minutes just sitting there over my lunch hour because there was no one there to meet me, and the office was closed. I saw this car drive up and just thought that I would let the man know that no one was in the office, and no one was answering the phone. Turns out, he was the property manager, and there had been a mix-up with another member of his staff.

He apologized profusely and took me to see what would be the layout of my new apartment. It was less money over the course of a year. It was a miracle sure enough!

Had I left a few minutes earlier and had I not stopped to tell that man that no one was around, I would have missed my blessing, my miracle, and God's provision.

On moving day, there were about thirteen dear friends who helped me move with all their cars, minivans, trailers, and SUVs. It took us two hours from start to finish. They were a miracle from God and part of His provision!

I learned many lessons from this little experience. He knew the storm would be there, He knew I would be freaking out, and He knew eventually I would come to the end of myself once again and eventually be quiet enough to be still. He knew my first reaction would be fear, panic, and self-centered confusion. He knew I would eventually sit down to look at the yearly costs and see no other way out. He knew it all. He knew when I would be looking up to the sky to see the rainbows, and He knew exactly when I would have had enough and chosen to leave during that lunch hour.

Clearly, He made the way. I praise Him and thank Him for His faithfulness to me even when my faith seems to be totally eclipsed by the circumstances that surround me.

Philippians 4:6 says, "Do not be anxious about anything, but in everything by prayer and petition, with thanksgiving, present your requests to God." Hopefully, next time, I will not be so anxious, scared, and worried but will, instead, be able rest in Him and know that His provision will be there *no matter what* these eyes may see or what it might look like to me! He is worthy, and He is my Jireh!

Remember that God loves you most and will provide for you no matter what storm you may be in the middle of in your imperfect life and know that it is always a perfect storm because it was designed by the only One who can make a way out of it for you!

Satan Works at My Office Building

She is a young twenty-something, normal-looking, miniskirt-wearing young professional. Her license plate on her demon mobile announces who she is and who she worships. The intricate flames start about halfway back the shiny black foundation. The dual exhaust pipes have pentagrams in the medium-sized circles at the end, which let the fumes escape from her car. Instead of the little metallic name of her particular brand of car, she has replaced it with 666.

The she-devil's car has become the topic of conversation in my cubicle section, my pod corner of the work world, on several occasions, which has always led to a discussion on witchcraft and evil. In a conversation, one cube mate thought that self-proclaimed witches are simply "self-deluded crazies." When I told him how local witches had made their way into my church and of the time when another friend at work was hiking and found animal sacrifice remnants in the local woods, he was somewhat shocked.

I informed him that the Wiccans and pagans clean the stretch of highway that my church property sets beside and have their very respectable blue Pennsylvania state signage on a local bypass. I told him of the "healing" witches in a local town and on a popular stretch of highway who hang out their shingles and have local businesses.

He replied, telling me that he thought witches were just fanatics who think they can wiggle their noses and make stuff happen. I assured him that they are not harmless delusionals who belong in the loony bin. I explained that the world would try to make him and everyone else think that there is nothing wrong with witchcraft or having a Satan-glorifying car, but that this is just another way in which evil has crept into our society.

The comment was made that some people are "good" witches, which is what most of the Wiccans would have you believe. I can assure you that there is nothing

---

good about witchcraft and the occult. While this "harmless, good witch" mentality seems acceptable enough to the world, there is a huge movement of this very type of evil, which is alive and well within this city and every city for that matter.

Even the Bible talks about the ones who practiced sorcery; and it talks about pagans, mediums, and oracles. Satan is not using anything new.

> For you have spent enough time in the past doing what pagans choose to do—living in debauchery, lust, drunkenness, orgies, carousing and detestable idolatry. (1 Peter 4:3)

> The acts of the sinful nature are obvious: sexual immorality, impurity and debauchery; idolatry and witchcraft; hatred, discord, jealousy, fits of rage, selfish ambition, dissensions, factions and envy; drunkenness, orgies, and the like. I warn you, as I did before, that those who live like this will not inherit the kingdom of God. (Galatians 5:19-21)

> Many of those who believed now came and openly confessed their evil deeds. A number who had practiced sorcery brought their scrolls together and burned them publicly. (Acts 19:18-19)

However, we, as believers, have a duty to call evil what it is *evil*. We must speak truth about the only Way, the only Truth, and life everlasting through Jesus Christ.

> Woe to those who call evil good and good evil, who put darkness for light and light for darkness, who put bitter for sweet and sweet for bitter. (Isaiah 5:20)

> As the old saying goes, "From evildoers come evil deeds." (1 Samuel 24:13)

> Do not set foot on the path of the wicked or walk in the way of evil men. (Proverbs 4:14)

> I write to you, fathers, because you have known Him who is from the beginning. I write to you, young men, because you have overcome the evil one. I write to you, dear children, because you have known the Father. (1 John 2:13)

Remember, you have the power to overcome the evil one in the mighty name of Jesus! We have a responsibility to tell unbelievers about the only way to the Father and the only way to their salvation!

THE RAINLESS RAINBOW: GOD'S MIRACLE BOW

I was walking back into work at the end of my lunch hour on Thursday, and there it was: the rainless rainbow. The sun was surrounded by a big circle of wispy clouds; and in a half circle, just above the sun, was a rainless rainbow—God's miracle bow.

It stopped me dead in my tracks, and I was fixated, staring at it. I had on my black shades, so it didn't even bother me to be looking just above the high afternoon sun. I tipped the shades to see if I could see it without them, and I could. There was a little circle kind of rainbow at the end of the half circle on the right side of it.

In my peripheral vision, I noticed a car had passed me and parked, Then I heard the clip-clop of high heels approaching me. There I stood, just looking at it, in awe!

Before she could ask me if something was wrong, I turned to her, a total stranger, and told her I was looking at the rainbow. She looked up in the same general direction and said she didn't see it. I said, "It's right there, right above the sun, in a half circle with the little circle there at the bottom of the right side—ROYGBIV!" Then I went through all the colors: red, orange, yellow, green, blue, indigo, and violet (my favorite).

She still didn't see it. So I handed her my shades and said, "Here, maybe you can see it with these." She took them and put them on and said that it was hurting her eyes to look up at the sun. When she had them on, she said she could see some sort of halo around the sun but did not see any rainbow. So then I went on and started blabbering, giving her more details about the location and the shape. She again said she saw the halo but no rainbow and handed me back my shades, and as she walked away, I said, "Wow, it is good to be a highly favored child of God! A rainbow only I can see!" I think she said "Must be," but I couldn't really hear her because she was walking away.

—

173

I stood there for a couple more minutes. It seemed like time stood still. I recounted the last two times I saw a rainbow: once when it really had just rained on my way to M's viewing and then one sun-filled, cold February morning when I was praying in my car before going into work.

For a few minutes, that felt like forever, it was just me and God and that rainless rainbow. So I walked back into work and started telling my office pod mates about the rainbow that only I could see and how God was so amazing.

I encourage you all today to keep looking up for your rainbow, the miracle bow that is meant just for you. Stay focused on God no matter what!

> God is not a man, that he should lie, nor a son of man, that he should change his mind. Does he speak and then not act? Does he promise and not fulfill? (Numbers 23:19)

> Now I am about to go the way of all the earth. You know with all your heart and soul that not one of all the good promises the Lord your God gave you has failed. Every promise has been fulfilled; not one has failed. (Joshua 23:14)

> I have sought your face with all my heart; be gracious to me according to your promise. (Psalms 119:58)

> Against all hope, Abraham in hope believed and so became the father of many nations, just as it had been said to him, "So shall your offspring be." Without weakening in his faith, he faced the fact that his body was as good as dead—since he was about a hundred years old—and that Sarah's womb was also dead. Yet he did not waver through unbelief regarding the promise of God, but was strengthened in his faith and gave glory to God, being fully persuaded that God had the power to do what he had promised. (Romans 4:18-21)

3:46 PM

I remember looking at the clock that day, focusing on the time. I had gotten an e-mail the night before saying that I would have a miracle at 3:46 PM.

At about 3:35 PM, my boss came to my desk and asked to see me in the conference room. I had expressed interest in a different position, more of a lateral move just that morning, so I figured she wanted to talk to me about it.

Here, my boss did share some amazing news with me regarding a project I had worked on. I got back to my desk right around 3:45 PM, and it was top-secret info. It was something I could not share with my coworkers.

However, the friend who sent me the 3:46 e-mail called and asked if anything happened. I couldn't tell her all the details just then with all the office ears listening, but I did confirm that something amazing did happen. There was much rejoicing when I left that day. Once I was alone in my car, tears of joy flowed, overflowing with gratitude for what God had done.

Remember nothing is impossible with God!

THOSE WHO HAVE NOT HEARD

I recently received an e-mail from my little brother who is seven years younger. I share a biological father with him and two other half siblings who are twins. I have very few memories of them as children or our father for that matter. Their mother recently informed me that I really only saw them maybe two, possibly a total of four times when I was a child before my adoption at twelve or thirteen years old.

My little brother had actually come to live with me during my last semester in nursing school. It was another example of my codependent, dysfunctional decision making. The last semester was the most stressful time in nursing school, and then I was trying to raise him, a teenage boy on top of that. He was in high school. I was crazy to think that I could have a positive impact on anyone else when I could not even take care of myself.

He is a part of my testimony, a testimony to the restoration that only God can provide between dysfunctional family members. He now lives in Alaska with his wife and their children, two nephews that I finally met. Both he and his wife are serving God as are the twins. Amen!

He wrote an e-mail, asking me questions about the many Native Americans in Alaska, and the question arose when he was witnessing to someone about the natives who die and have not heard the Gospel or don't know anything about Jesus. What happens to them? What happens to those who have not heard or had the opportunity to hear the good news?

I pondered on this and set about to find the scripture that would give him God's answer on the matter. I found Hebrews 11:6:

> And without faith it is impossible to please God, because anyone who comes to Him must believe that he exists and that he rewards those who earnestly seek Him.

The scripture really says it all: that to please God, we must believe that He exists, that He rewards those who earnestly seek Him, and that we need to have faith in our belief. It seems simple enough.

In every culture across all of time, there is a spiritual need to worship something higher than ourselves. God made us spiritual beings after all.

However, the Native Americans are pantheistic. Pantheism, in plain Julie translation, means they have the eagle, the bear, the trees, etc. To them, it is all God. Their religion is also wrapped in their culture just like hedonism (the philosophy that pleasure is the most important pursuit of mankind) is wrapped in the pervasive culture of the world.

I think what the scripture, in Hebrews, was trying to say was that to acknowledge that He is God, the one true living God, is the key. Then there is also the scripture that talks about how they die because they have no knowledge.

There is an element of God's supernatural nature that I don't think we here on earth will really ever be able to understand with regard to what happens after physical death, or what happens if you die and you have never heard the plan of salvation. I'm not sure that I have really found an answer, and maybe I only have more questions.

However, I do know what I believe, and I know it is my duty to spread the news through the land. I also know that, once you hear the plan of salvation, you are responsible for having received that knowledge.

The question that was posed really drives home the point that the Great Commission is so important. We must take forth the Gospel and the message of Jesus's salvation for all mankind, as this is really our essential task as believers, so that all would have the opportunity to hear and know God.

Even here in the Lower 48, as the Alaskans call it, where virtually all households have at least one TV or, at the very least, a radio or a computer, it seems unlikely that there are those who have not heard, but I know they are here. They are *everywhere*: our neighbors, our mechanics, our grocery clerks, our bank tellers, our waiters, our friends, our family members. They are everyday people walking around who have no idea who Jesus is and what He really did just for them.

I would even go so far as to say that there are believers, people who believe Jesus is the Son of God, who have no idea what Jesus really did just for them either. There are the people who believe in God but don't go to church and people who sit in church, week after week in the pews, and really have no idea that their salvation is personal.

Our salvation is a gift, and the gift is freely given. It is up to us to choose it or reject it. If we accept it, it is again our choice if we will go forth and tell others.

—

Luke 23:42 is the verse where the criminal on the cross, beside our Redeemer, said to Him, "Jesus, remember me when You come into Your kingdom." Jesus told him that he would join Him in paradise that very day. The criminal knew that he was going to die. Most of us won't be so lucky, and tomorrow is never promised.

So I would encourage anyone—who does not have a personal relationship with God the Father, the Son, and the Holy Spirit and who may be reading this—to make the choice today and accept the gift of Jesus's salvation. He died for you and for your sins, all of them. No matter how horrible you may think they are, He has it all covered. It is as simple as asking Jesus into your heart, believing in Him, and being sorry for the things you have done wrong, and being willing to be changed and to be healed. If you decide to make that choice, I would encourage you to find someone who is a believer and talk to him about the next steps.

For the believers, I would encourage you to share your faith in your actions and in your words but know that your actions will speak louder.

FOREVER-EVER?

There are so many references regarding time in the Bible. For instance, in Genesis 21:2 it says, "Sarah became pregnant and bore a son to Abraham in his old age, at the very time God had promised him." Joshua 22:3 says, "For a long time now—to this very day—you have not deserted your brothers but have carried out the mission the Lord your God gave you." Mark 1:15 says, "'The time has come,' he said. 'The kingdom of God is near. Repent and believe the good news.'"

From this time, in the old time, at the appointed time, for a time, harvest time . . . ticktock . . . ticktock. It just never ceases to make me pause when meditating about God and His time.

So many scriptures and worship choruses also talk about forever. Forever? My finite mind can just not grasp how long forever really is. Forever-ever?

Second Samuel 7:25 reads, "And now, Lord God, keep forever the promise you have made concerning your servant and his house. Do as you promised." First Chronicles 16:34 says, "Give thanks to the Lord, for he is good; his love endures forever."

Science can do studies—carbon dating and speed-of-light testing—to try to measure time, to try to quantify time; but God's time and concept of it is just not ours. How long is forever? His time—how fast or slow is the twinkling of an eye? How did *He* stretch time?

God's time is simply God's time much like how His thoughts are not our thoughts and *His* ways are not our ways. Remember that, no matter what you are waiting for, God's timing is best. God sees forever and knows the beginning and ending of all things.

This requires patience, which is why I believe patience is a fruit of the Spirit. It is just not a natural thing to be patient, to be still, and to wait on God.

Take heart in this gem in Hebrews for some encouragement.

You need to persevere so that when you have done the will of God,
you will receive what he has promised. (Hebrews 10:36, NIV)

This following verse in Philippians encourages us to persevere and focus on the true goal our existence.

I press on toward the goal to win the prize for which God has called
me heavenward in Christ Jesus. (Philippians 3:14)

Press on and press in and rest in God's sovereignty and in the fact that His time is not ours, and that forever is in His Hands.

FEAR AND YEAST BUDS

So they brought him. When the spirit saw Jesus, it immediately threw the boy into a convulsion. He fell to the ground and rolled around, foaming at the mouth. Jesus asked the boy's father, "How long has he been like this?" "From childhood," he answered. "It has often thrown him into fire or water to kill him. But if you can do anything, take pity on us and help us." "If you can?" said Jesus. "Everything is possible for Him who believes." Immediately the boy's father exclaimed, "I do believe; help me overcome my unbelief!"
—Mark 9:20-24, The Healing of a Boy with an Evil Spirit

If it was possible for Jesus to be attitudinal, I'm guessing that this would have been one of those times. He rhetorically asks the father of this boy, "*If* I can?!" I can hear the holy indignation or righteous anger that Jesus must have felt. He had, just a few verses earlier, admonished them all.

"O unbelieving generation," Jesus replied, "how long shall I stay with you? How long shall I put up with you?" (Mark 9:19)

This incident is just after the Transfiguration where Jesus went up on a mountain with Peter, James, and John. His clothes became white, and He talked with Moses and Elijah. I'm sure Jesus, or at least the fully human part of Him, wanted to blurt out, "Hello, I was just conversing (*platicar* for my Spanish brothers and sisters) with Moses and Elijah. Are you for real? *If* I can do anything? *If?*"

I love Jesus's answer to this desperate man because He was fully God: *Everything is possible for him who believes!* Chew on that promise of the Word for a few minutes. Feed upon it, ingest it, digest it, and let it soak into every fiber of your being and nourish your soul. Jesus said *everything*!

How often do we treat God the same way as this poor father did?

"Well, God, if you could uh maybe just help me out a little bit, if you could possibly uh help . . ." Often we start with some pansy prayers and requests, acting like He really can't do what we are asking. We should be coming boldly to the throne in faith!

I also love the father's response. He tells Jesus that he does believe and asks for help with his unbelief! How often do we believe? But then, that fleshy side rears its ugly head, and that little glimmer of doubt shines through just like that one little particle of yeast that makes the whole loaf rise. That one little yeast bud of unbelief and doubt can affect your whole life and the way you live it.

I think, sometimes, my own unbelief comes from my fear. Fear strengthens doubt, and Satan will feed upon that and rejoice in your moment of unbelief.

I pray that we can all move and walk in our faith and certainty in Him, away from fear, doubt, and unbelief. I'm praying for God to help me in my unbelief too! Would you live differently if you didn't have unbelief within you?

Remember that everything is possible with God! Take that step of faith toward belief in the only One worthy!

ENDING PRAYER

If you don't know God as well as you would like, don't know Jesus as your personal Savior, or just want to rededicate your life and all that you are, I encourage you to pray the following prayer:

Lord,

I come humbly before You and bow down before You to give You the honor that You rightly deserve. You are mighty and merciful. You are so great, and greatly to be praised! Your goodness knows no limits, and I am grateful that You created me.

I acknowledge that I need You in my heart, in my mind, in my life, in all things, and at all times. I accept the gift of your salvation and invite Jesus into my heart in a deeper way.

I know and accept that I cannot save myself, and that it is only by Jesus's blood, His death on the cross, and resurrection that I am saved at all. I ask for the forgiveness of all my sins and pray that You cleanse the very depths of my soul.

Make me new and reveal to me your purpose and plan for my life. I need your Living Water and your Living Word to quench my thirsty soul. I am nothing without You, and I can be nothing without You.

Send your counselor, your Comforter, to teach me and heal my heart, my mind, and my soul. Please give me right thinking, wisdom, understanding, and knowledge.

—

I consecrate my life, every part of my being, to You for Your holy plan. I submit and yield my will and seek after Your perfect will for my life. I commit my life and all that I am to You. I trust that You love me, will provide for me, will never leave me, and have my best interest in mind.

Let me be born again and be found in You to serve You. Let me have a deeper relationship with You that grows stronger everyday.

Let me love You and pour my praise upon Your feet like oil. I will worship You and You alone. Let me focus on You and let me feel Your perfect love.

Be the Lord in my life, be my Savior, be my everything! Amen!

I love you all, but remember God loves you most!

Jewels